Practical Pruning

OTHER BARRON'S GARDENING BOOKS

House Plants
How To Grow Better Roses
Making and Planning a Small Garden
Simple Plant Propagation
Simple Vegetable Growing
The Perfect Lawn
How To Grow and Use Herbs
Simple Tomato Growing
Making the Most of Your Greenhouse

Practical Pruning

Edited by
Roger Grounds

BARRON'S/Woodbury New York

First published in Great Britain in
1974 by Ward Lock Limited, 116 Baker Street,
London, W1M 2BB, a member of the Pentos Group

Designed by John Munday

Text filmset in Times Roman (327/344)

International Standard Book Number 0–8120–0797–2
Library of Congress Catalog Card Number 77–70395

American Edition Published in 1977 by
Barron's Educational Series, Inc.
113 Crossways Park Drive
Woodbury, New York 11797

Printed and bound by
Cox & Wyman Ltd
London, Fakenham and Reading

Contents

Using loppers to remove shoots from a rose that would be too tough for secateurs (pruning shears). More shears are ruined by using them to cut wood that is too thick or too tough for them than by any other type of misuse.

Introduction

To prune or not to prune? This is a question that always seems to face gardeners. Most feel they ought, but are not sure why or how. It is accepted practice for the orchard, fairly frequently carried out in the rose garden but rather haphazard elsewhere. Most often it is only performed when a shrub or tree begins to encroach on its neighbour, a path or a building.

Pruning is often looked upon as the answer to make a barren tree fruitful. Carried out correctly, it will—eventually! Years of neglect cannot be rectified in one season. The unknowing pruner who cuts because he thinks he ought but does not know how, often finishes up with no flowers at all through too hard pruning or carrying out the operation at the wrong time of year.

Some gardeners are obsessed by tidiness and formality, wanting their trees and shrubs to be like smart soldiers on parade. Trees are lopped to a standard height, whilst for shrubs out come the clippers and branches and twigs are cut back to a predetermined size and shape, all identical. As spring advances, the gardener becomes distraught for he has not allowed for the different angles or rates of growth that now reduce his parade-ground effect to a shambles. Strict uniformity is in any case acceptable only in the parterre which is laid out in symmetrical geometric designs where lines have to be kept sharp.

What then is pruning? Why does one prune? When? How?

Pruning can be described as the removal of a part or parts of a woody plant by man for a specific purpose. The reasons for pruning are:
1. To train the plant.
2. To maintain plant health.
3. To obtain a balance between growth and flowering.
4. To improve the quality of flowers, fruit, foliage or stems.
5. To restrict growth.

Training A woody plant will come into cropping earlier if it is allowed to grow naturally. Pruning delays flowering but in the early years it ensures a framework of strong well-spaced branches, later to produce flowers and fruit. A tree of desired size and shape can be fashioned which is not only well balanced and delightful to the eye but carries flowers or fruits where they can be easily seen and reached. Building up of the initial framework makes for easier management of tree, shrub or climber in later years.

Maintenance of plant health A beautiful tree is a healthy one!

Control of pests and diseases is essential and it is easiest if the cause of these afflictions can be removed as early as possible. Pruning is one way in which this can be done. In early years, pests and diseases interfere with training; in an aged specimen they hasten the end, whilst at all stages of growth they are unsightly, can destroy flowers or fruit and weaken branches—the fall of a large branch can mean severe damage or death to the tree.

Routine spraying can control pests and some diseases in shrubs and young trees but it becomes impracticable if not impossible on large trees, when pruning is the only feasible method of control. Most diseases that attack trees enter through wounds and spread via the conducting tissue, killing off branches as they extend their hold. If disease reaches the trunk death usually results. The disease organism travels beyond the wood it has killed off and its presence in apparently healthy wood can be detected by a brown interior staining. When diseased wood is being removed always cut back to sound wood, that is, wood where there is no staining.

Dead wood is always unsightly and likely to break off, causing damage. It is the breeding ground for disease which can spread from the dead wood to the live (eg coral spot). When removing any wood include also that which is dead.

Maintaining a balance between growth and flowering A tree or shrub in strong active growth produces few flowers and in fact too heavy pruning can delay or even prevent flowering. Pruning in the early years should be sufficient only for training.

Once a tree has come into full flowering, shoot production will decline until at maturity very little annual growth is being added. In a mature plant it is the young wood which produces leaves and in many plants even the flowers, whilst with age the quality of these and the rate at which they are produced declines. It is therefore desirable to encourage a woody plant to maintain the production of young wood by judicious pruning.

Improvement of quality of flowers, fruit, foliage and stems The more flowers and fruit a plant produces, the smaller they become, as can be witnessed on an unpruned rosebush or fruit tree. Pruning reduces the amount of wood and so diverts energy into the production of larger, though fewer, flowers and/or fruit. The length of flower spikes on an unpruned butterfly bush *Buddleia davidii* may be 4in but can exceed 12in on one that has been hard pruned.

Leaves are produced only on current season's growth. The more vigorous this is the larger will be the leaves, and in plants with coloured leaves the more intense will be the colouring. Shrubs grown for their foliage, summer or autumn, variegated, coloured or dissected, are pruned hard annually.

Some deciduous shrubs have coloured barks which are especially delightful in winter. The best colour is produced on young stems and the greatest length and most intense colour results from hard pruning.

Restriction of growth Trees and shrubs left to develop naturally, grow bigger and bigger, becoming an embarrassment where space is restricted and so pruning becomes necessary to keep them within bounds.

Other forms of pruning There are some jobs carried out in a garden which are also forms of pruning although they are not always recognized as such. The cutting of flowers from woody plants for home decoration is a type of pruning.

9

Trimming of hedges is restrictive pruning applied to a row of shrubs. Topiary, the clipping of bushes to bizarre shapes, is a combination of training and restrictive pruning, and so is pleaching, used to make living screens or arches. Tree surgery is an extreme form of pruning used to maintain a tree in a healthy condition.

Salix alba, one of the most spectacular of the willows grown for their winter bark, shown in the first picture. To achieve this, the plant needs to be pruned really hard each spring (second picture).

a   b

1
Training Pruning

Most trees and shrubs grown in a garden are purchased from a nursery. It is useful for the reader to know how these were raised for it does have some bearing on pruning.

Woody plants may be on their own roots, having been raised from seed, cuttings or layers; or they may have a root system (rootstock) of one plant and the aerial part (scion) of another as a result of grafting (budding is but one form of grafting). Grafting is used to propagate trees and shrubs because:

1. It is the most reliable or only method of increase.
2. By use of a selected rootstock it is possible to regulate the ultimate size of tree, eg as in fruit trees.
3. It is possible to produce artificial types of trees, eg shrubs can be made into trees or pendulous shrubs can become weeping standards.
4. It can induce earlier flowering, eg grafted tree magnolias flower earlier than those raised from seed.

Trees may be grafted low, with their union close to the ground, or they may be high grafted on to stems of varying lengths. When planting, those that are grafted low should have their union buried unless the rootstock governs the ultimate size of the tree, as with flowering crabs on apple rootstocks; these are planted with their union well above ground-level.

Remember that grafted trees and shrubs are always likely to produce suckers from their rootstocks, and these, if left,

11

grow away at the expense of the scion variety. Suckers should be removed as soon as they appear. Do not cut off at ground-level otherwise all buds below will start into growth and where there was one sucker there will now be several. Scrape away the soil until the point of origin is exposed, then with a sharp downward pull remove the sucker; this takes away the basal buds which cutting would have left.

Rooted cuttings, layers and graded seedlings are lined out in nursery rows and grown on for a year, by which time some of the shrubs may be ready for selling. The rest of the shrubs and the trees are grown on until they are big enough for sale.

Trees are trained in two main ways: as standards which have

Pruning of different types of standard trees. The tree on the left has its leading shoot pinched out, and will produce a branching head: the tree on the right is left with its leading shoot and will develop into a more or less pyramidal tree.

a clear 6ft stem on top of which the framework is allowed to develop; and as central leaders where the leader is continuous, with branches arising all the way along the length of trunk. Standards are the form most commonly offered for sale by nurseries and are well suited to small-growing trees such as crab apples and mountain ash. But for the larger-growing trees the central leader should be used.

Training

Deciduous specimens Sold most often in nurseries as bare-rooted, these should be soaked in water prior to firm planting and to the same depth as in the nursery. Grafted specimens should be planted with their union just below ground-level. Following planting, select and retain three or five of the strongest shoots, cutting back side shoots to two or three buds and reducing their length by about a half. This should encourage new shoots to develop near to ground-level in the following growing season; in the next winter these main stems are cut back again to half of their new growth. At the same time the centre of the bush is opened up by removing crossing branches and any clutter of short shoots. Cut back the remaining side shoots to two or three buds and thin where crowded so as to produce a well-balanced, evenly spaced framework.

Evergreens Sold either as balled specimens or as container-grown, these are planted in spring to the same depth as they were in the nursery, having first been given a good soaking. Select the three strongest shoots, reducing the remainder, and lightly tip or remove their growing points. In the following spring, thin out crowded branches and open up the centre of the bush.

a

b

c

Training pruning of young feathered trees. The first picture shows the removal of the lower branches, the second picture the shortening of the laterals to encourage the stem to thicken, and the third picture the removal of a developing double-leader.

14

2
Pruning
of Established Trees
and Shrubs

As an annual operation and prior to any kind of pruning a number of basic tasks must be performed. All dead, damaged and diseased wood, and suckers at their point of origin, must be removed from grafted plants. Crossing branches and thin crowded shoots should be cut out, and thin weak shoots removed completely or cut hard back. Shoots which are showing reversion, a common complaint with the foliage of variegated plants and an occasional occurrence with flower colour, eg in camellias, should have the offending branch traced back to its point of origin and removed. All these tasks should be carried out in the spring.

Pruning of established shrubs

The method and timing of pruning deciduous shrubs is governed by the age of the wood on which flowering takes place: this may be on current season's growth, or on one-year-old wood or spurs. Evergreens and tender plants are considered separately, and so also is pruning carried out for a special effect.

Shrubs flowering on current season's growth   Growth has to be made before flowering can take place so shrubs within this group tend to flower in summer and autumn. If left unpruned, shrubs grow higher but with reduced vigour, more flowers are produced but these are smaller and poorer in quality. Hard pruning means the removal of a large amount of wood so that the energy of the bush is diverted to fewer shoots and flowers which are consequently larger and of better quality.

Pruning is carried out when bushes are dormant, during the winter months. Weather permitting, January or February are the best months. All shoots are cut back hard to within two or three buds of ground-level or a framework.

Another method is to cut half the shoots back to two or three buds and the remainder to a half or third of their length. Hard pruning delays flowering but with this treatment the flowering period can be extended and the quality of flowers is still high. The following winter these longer shoots are removed completely; some thinning of resultant shoots is beneficial in spring.

When shrubs of this nature flower in flushes or flower continuously, dead-heading should be practised to improve their appearance and to prevent them expending energy on ripening fruit. This consists of the removal of the dead flower and if possible two or three buds on the flower stem; cutting is to be preferred, for though some stems can be easily broken

The pruning of shrubs which flower on the current season's growth. The object is to remove those shoots which have already flowered.

off, others sustain damage to neighbouring buds.

Strong growth and good quality flowers following hard pruning depend upon a plentiful food supply, so apply a base dressing of a general fertiliser at the rate of 2–4oz per sq yd, the heavier dressing for old and well-established shrubs.

Shrubs flowering on one-year-old wood Growth is made in one growing season and in the following year flowers are produced either on this growth or on short laterals coming from it. This group tends to flower in the early part of the year. Individual shrubs can be pruned directly after flowering, or pruning can be delayed until summer when all the shrubs in the garden falling within this group can be treated; if berries are to be a feature pruning takes place in early spring.

Shrubs in this group can be left unpruned but they tend to become too tall, encroach on their neighbours or create an unmanageable tangle of growth. Pruning then consists of removing the twigs which have flowered. If young growth is breaking, cut back to where there is a strong young shoot growing in the desired direction. Thin out the remainder of the shoots, especially opening up the centre of the bush so as to improve air movement which will help to ripen the wood.

The pruning of shrubs which flower on one-year-old wood. The shoot which has flowered is removed, leaving the new growth to flower next season.

Unripe wood is especially a problem during a wet season when growth is lush. In summer of such a year, carry out a further thinning to help ripen wood. As less wood is removed in the pruning of this group smaller applications of a general fertilizer are required. This can be at the rate of 1–2oz per sq yd annually, or double the rate every second year.

Shrubs flowering on spurs A spur can be described as a branch, usually a short one, which will produce its flower buds on one-year-old wood but will continue each year to produce more on the same branch; sometimes the wood has to be two years old before flower buds are produced but new flower buds continue to be added in subsequent years. These shrubs grow strongly in their early years, producing few flowers, but as growth slows down, so spurs begin to form naturally and there

Forsythia flowers on wood of the previous season's growth. To ensure an abundance of this type of growth it should be pruned hard immediately after flowering.

a

is a reduction of extension growth. When this stage is reached, pruning can almost cease.

Pruning may need to be practised during the early years of development, especially if space is limited. Once a framework has been formed all annual stems are cut back to three or four buds, with the exception of the leading shoot on main branches. The following year some of these buds will grow away, and if the others do not flower they will form flower buds to produce blossom in the next year. Once these flower buds form, any growth which develops beyond them should be removed.

Evergreens Their main attraction in the garden is their foliage in the winter months. Most evergreens are liable to damage if exposed to cold winds or subject to prolonged low temperatures when the ground stays frozen for long periods. This shows itself by death of branches or the discoloration and death of leaves. Pruning of evergreens is carried out in spring just before growth commences. Cut out any winter-damaged wood, trimming back discoloured foliage; thin and trim to shape. If evergreens are also grown for their flowers, they invariably produce these on one-year wood and so pruning of these is delayed until after flowering.

Tender plants As these are always liable to damage by frost

b   c

pruning is delayed until spring when the danger of severe frost has passed. Those flowering on one-year-old wood are not pruned until after flowering. Pruning consists of the removal of winter damage, removal of stalks which have carried flowers and some thinning.

Pruning for special effects Shrubs are not always grown in gardens for flowers and fruit; sometimes stems or bark or leaves have more appeal.

Shrubs such as the *Cornus alba* forms or the coloured osiers

19

Salix alba forms are planted for the effect of their colourful bark during the winter months. Bark colour is most intense on young wood and the best effect is from the strong young shoots that result from hard pruning. *Cornus*, *Kerria* and *Rubus*, and others with a suckering habit, are cut down to ground-level in spring. Those which do not have this habit are treated rather differently. Several leaders are permitted, each of which is feathered so as to expose the lower part of the stems at an early age.

Many shrubs have more attractive foliage, either summer or autumn, than flowers. Leaves are only produced on current season's growth and those of the largest size are on the strongest growth. Deciduous shrubs with variegated, coloured or cut foliage are pruned hard almost to ground-level or to a framework during the winter months and fed copiously.

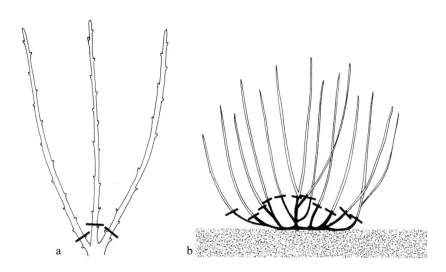

a

b

Coppicing or hard pruning, to achieve a sub-tropical foliage effect. This type of pruning is only suitable for one or two trees such as *Ailanthus glandulosa* or *Paulownia tomentosa*. The latter, when treated this way and grown in rich soil, will produce huge heart-shaped leaves up to 3ft across [a].

Pruning for bark effect. In this case the pruning is of the type used for those plants whose young growth produces colourful bark in winter. These include several *Cornus* species and several willows (*Salix* species) [b].

20

3
Climbers
and Wall Shrubs

Climbers are plants with weak stems that take themselves up towards the light by means of their climbing habit. Plants have adapted themselves to this habit in a number of different ways:

1. by twining stems, as in wisteria,
2. by twining leaf stalks, as in clematis,
3. by tendrils, as with the vines *Vitis* species,
4. by tendrils producing pads that stick to their supports, as happens in the Virginia creeper *Parthenocissus tricuspidata*,
5. by roots produced on aerial stems which stick to their support, the best example being the common ivy *Hedera helix*,
6. by thorns which hook on to support, as in climbing roses.

In addition there are plants, lax of habit, that get themselves up to the light by flopping over rocks, trees or other shrubs.

In the garden climbers can be used for a number of purposes: for covering pergolas, walls and fences; for training up poles; and for growing over or through trees and shrubs. One chooses the climber most suitable for a particular site. On a bare wall or fence only a climber that sticks itself to its support can be used, but if the wall or fence is provided with a trellis or parallel wires any kind of climber can be grown.

Supports for climbers

Trellises should be securely fixed in position after having been painted or treated with wood preservative prior to erection. The thickness of timber to be used depends on the type of plant it has to support. Strong climbers such as wisteria produce heavy stems, so strong supports are necessary. Metal trellising can be used as long as it has been painted or galvanized and, again, the heaviest gauge is necessary for the strongest climbers. If climbers are going to be grown against wooden buildings or fences that will need painting periodically, it is advisable to fix the trellises to their support with hinges so that they can be swung away at painting time.

Parallel wires are quite suitable and easier than trellising to install and maintain; they should be of a sufficiently heavy gauge to support the climbers and galvanized, painted or covered with plastic. Fix them to the wall horizontally, with

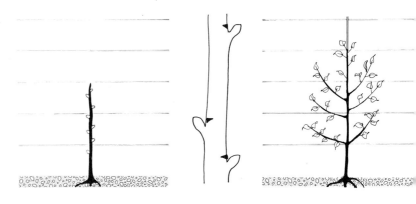

The training of climbers. The first illustration shows the plant in spring of its 1st year after planting, showing where the shoots should be nicked. The second illustration is a close-up showing precisely where the shoots need to be nicked. The purpose of nicking is to make the buds grow out more horizontally than they would otherwise. The next illustration shows the plant having made

9–12in between them, through eyebolts with strainers at each end to keep the wires taut. Upright canes, vertical strings or wires, are often added to give extra support.

Trees make admirable supports for strong-growing climbers. The trees should be mature, but even dead trees can be used; in fact if there is a dead or unsightly tree in the garden which cannot be removed, the best thing to do is to hide it behind a climber. Dead trees should have their smaller branches removed and with live trees it is advisable to reduce the canopy to admit more light. After planting the climber insert a cane or fix vertical wires to take the stems up into the branches of the tree.

Pergolas again need strong climbers that get their stems up on top of the structure as quickly as possible. The reduced light from the top cover causes lower leaves to fall, resulting in bare stems near to ground-level, but selected climbers can be planted in to hide the bareness and introduce some colour lower down.

Supporting poles may be of trimmed timber, cut tree branches or metal. Wooden poles need to be treated with wood preservative, at least at their bases, and metal posts must

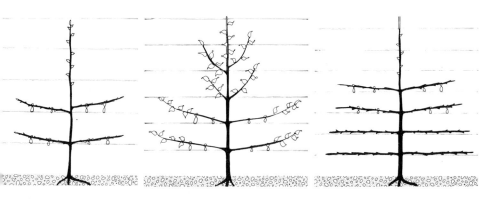

growth following nicking. The following picture shows the shoot being tied down to the supporting canes in spring of the 2nd year, and the nicking of the buds on the new leader. The next illustration shows growth made during the 2nd growing season and the last illustration shows a tree being tied down and nicked again in spring in the 3rd year after planting.

be painted or galvanized to prevent rusting. Grow the weaker climbers on poles, or be sure to prune each year so that there is never more growth than the poles can support.

When shrubs are to act as supports, choose those that are well established, reasonably vigorous and of moderate size. Select climbers which are not themselves of vigorous growth and be prepared to be ruthless with them at pruning time so

23

that the supporting shrub is not smothered.

Planting climbers

Climbers are now almost always container-grown and on sale throughout the year. Spring planting is the best, but planting can be done throughout much of the year as long as attention is paid to watering until the climber is established. After planting, reduce the stems to a half or even a third of their original lengths to encourage young growth to develop at or

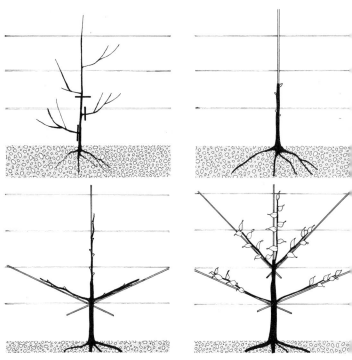

near to ground-level. Select three or five of the strongest shoots, provide them with canes, vertical wires or strings, and train them in the desired direction of the permanent support. At the end of the next growing season reduce all the leaders by about a half, cutting the weakest shoots even harder; thin out crowded shoots and space well on the main stems. Repeat each year until the allotted space has been filled with a well-

24

spaced framework.

Regular attention is necessary in the training of climbers, and when growth is in spate they need almost daily attention. Clematis and other plants that have twining leaf stalks, if neglected even for a week, produce an unmanageable tangle which defies the patience of Job to unravel. Moreover, if climbers that stick to their supports either by roots or sucker pads are allowed to wander in the wrong direction, it means that the shoots must be pulled off whatever surface they have fastened on and they will not stick again.

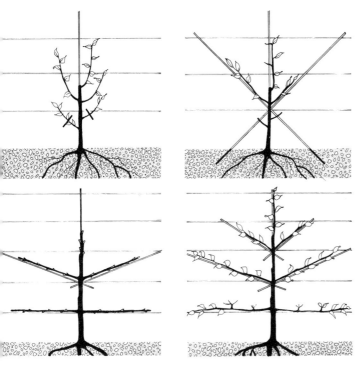

A sequence showing the use of canes in the training of a woody plant which is required to grow flat against a wall. The operation is described in detail in the text.

Evergreens are treated similarly to deciduous climbers but pruning is always less severe, the growth being tipped rather than cut hard back. Do ensure that the bases of walls and fences are adequately clothed to start with and keep them so.

Established pruning for climbers

The same rules apply to established pruning for climbers as

for shrubs, that is the method and timing is dependent on the age of the wood on which flowers are produced. Those which flower on **current season's growth** can be cut hard back to an established framework during the winter. More often they are cut to ground-level and in this case all the training pruning described in the earlier part of this chapter can be ignored. When pruned hard, flowering is delayed, but the flowering season may be extended by leaving in some shoots which are trimmed but not cut hard; these are removed completely in the following year. Very late flowering climbers in this group, or in areas where early frosts are prevalent, are cut much less severely, growth being reduced by about half and this removed completely in the following winter.

Climbers flowering on **previous season's wood** are pruned after flowering. Shoots which have flowered are removed or cut back to where new growth is developing, and thinning out of remaining growth follows. Train in new shoots as they develop, keeping only enough to comfortably furnish; any surplus should be removed.

After a framework has been formed, the **spur producers** have all side shoots cut back to two or three buds during February. For some this treatment may have to be carried out twice, once in summer when shoots are cut to form fine buds and again in winter when any resulting growth is shortened back to two or three.

Climbers on poles need drastic pruning at all times, irrespective of the group to which they belong, to ensure that no more growth is permitted than the poles can support. **Climbers on trees**, on the other hand, need no further pruning once they are established, unless growth becomes excessive and threatens the tree or if a clutter of dead wood occurs. **On pergolas** pruning is minimal, just thinning out to prevent overcrowding and removing shoots which wave about in the wind and annoy people passing beneath. Some training in of young growth should be practised so that periodically some of the oldest stems can be removed.

Siting and planting of wall shrubs

An area close to a wall is more protected than one in the open, and of course drier. In summer walls absorb as well as reflect

26

heat and so, being warm and dry, help to ripen wood.

A south wall is the warmest and driest and well suited to growing plants considered to be tender or needing to have their wood thoroughly ripened to flower freely. A west wall is almost as good. An east wall, however, is not suitable for early-flowering shrubs; flowers of many plants can withstand some freezing without damage as long as they can thaw out slowly, but winter or early spring flowers are likely to be damaged in the early morning sunshine on an east wall. Such a wall is better suited for the growing of sprawling or climbing plants than for plants considered to be tender.

On a north wall there is no direct sun, and so it remains moister with less fluctuation of temperature, hence cooler than a more open position. A north wall, therefore, is well suited to shade lovers and shrubs requiring cool, moist growing conditions in summer.

When there are south or west walls in the garden it is possible to be more adventurous in the choice of plants and to try out trees or shrubs which are classed as tender in a particular district for growing in the open. Shrubs which, when grown in the open, flower sparsely or not at all, especially after a wet summer when wood fails to ripen properly, often flower profusely against a wall. West and south walls offer protection to shrubs that flower in the winter months by allowing flowers to develop fully and remain open and undamaged by the cold.

Shrubs for planting against a wall may be offered bare-rooted, balled in the case of evergreens, but many, and especially the tender ones, are now sold in containers. Planting is best carried out just before growth starts, which will be early spring for some deciduous shrubs but in most cases mid-spring is preferable. Plant firmly, 9–12in away from the wall, and finish up with a shallow depression in the soil around the main stem so as to facilitate watering, which should continue until the shrubs are well established—on each occasion giving a good soaking.

Training wall shrubs Wall plants which are naturally trees can be trained to a single leader. A single-stemmed young plant should be chosen and headed back in spring to about 9in above the lowest wire or 2ft from the ground if on a trellis.

27

Insert a strong cane or fix a vertical wire, up which the leader is to be trained.

In the following growing season, the uppermost buds will develop. Select the strongest and train in as a new leader. Take the next two shoots and tie one on either side of the leader to canes fixed in position at an angle of 45° to the vertical; any surplus shoots are stopped at four buds. In the following spring, lower the branches to an angle of 60° (keeping the side branches at an angle allows extension growth to develop). Meanwhile the leader is beheaded at 9in above the next wire or about 18in above the first pair of branches when growing on a trellis. The strongest shoot is again tied in as the leader, and two more are tied in at 45° whilst surplus shoots are stopped at four buds. In the following spring again, the bottom pair of branches is brought to the horizontal, the second tier dropped to 60°, surplus shoots stopped at four buds and the leader again beheaded.

This practice continues until the uppermost wire or the top of the trellis is reached, after which the leader can be allowed to grow on. In the summer of the following year, the leader is then removed just above the top tier.

Once the bottom tier has been tied in horizontally, flowering can be allowed to take place. At all times any branches coming away from the wall are removed.

The above method may be slow but it builds up a well-balanced framework, provides good cover low down and flowering is progressive.

The following is a simpler method, best suited for deciduous subjects, and while not as good as the one just described it produces results more quickly and still provides reasonable cover. On a single-stemmed young plant, cut a notch just above the buds that you wish to form branches in spring. This forces those buds into growth which is allowed to develop untied whilst the leader is tied to a central cane or wire. In the following springtime, the best-placed side branches are pulled down towards the wire and secured near the leader but not tied so tightly as to lie at the horizontal. Any surplus shoots are cut back to two or three buds. Notching again is carried out and the resulting shoots are allowed to grow freely whilst the leader is secured to its vertical support. In the next year,

28

prior to growth starting, the lowest branches resulting from the first year's notching are pulled down and tied at the horizontal. Those resulting from the previous year's notching are again tied loosely. This continues up to the top of the wall when the treatment of the leader as already described is repeated.

Another method of training a tree, which is also well suited to most shrubs, is to produce a fan-trained framework. Plant a single-stemmed young plant and make a cut 3ft from ground-level. Insert four canes, the lower pair at 45° and the upper at about 30° from the vertical, two on either side of the main stem. When growth starts, select the strongest four shoots and train up the canes, tying in at regular intervals. When planting a branched shrub select four stems and remove the remainder. Just prior to the commencement of the next growing season, cut back these four shoots to a third of their original length. Of the shoots produced, select two from each stem and tie to suitably fixed wires or strings, pinching back the remainder. At the end of the next growing season there will probably be a sufficient framework built up for shrubs, after which established pruning can begin.

Trees will need another season to complete the framework. Prior to the commencement of growth, all the leaders are reduced to about half of the length of wood produced in the previous season. Of the resulting growth select only two shoots, pinching back the remainder. Space these out and tie into position; if there are too many shoots any that are crowded can be removed completely. Now that the framework is complete, established pruning can commence.

Established pruning of weak shrubs

Tender shrubs and trees, especially evergreens, are usually allowed to develop with the minimum of pruning. In May cut out any winter damage, thin out crowded shoots, remove old flower stalks and cut back any shoots coming away from the wall. The same rules apply to tender shrubs as to all others, except that pruning is usually carried out later, that is, in spring when the danger of frost has passed.

Deciduous trees and shrubs flowering on current season's

29

growth can be cut hard back to the framework although some young stems are left unpruned apart from a light tipping.

The pruning of **deciduous trees and shrubs flowering on previous year's growth** is delayed until after flowering, when that growth which has flowered is removed, cutting back where possible to where new growth is breaking. Of the new growth, select only enough shoots to comfortably fill the available space and remove the rest. Those which are **spur bearing** will have all young shoots shortened back to two or three buds until a spur system has built up.

Irrespective of the type of pruning, periodically train in some new shoots into the framework so as to be able occasionally to remove some of the oldest wood.

4
Roses

Roses are occasionally raised on their own roots but in the main are grafted. Those on their own roots include a few climbers, shrubs or species roses raised from cuttings, though most species are raised from seed; in all of these shoots coming from below ground-level can be allowed to remain, for none will be suckers.

Removal of suckers

Most roses offered for sale are grafted, having a root system different from the aerial part of the plant. These roses may produce suckers and the gardener must be on the alert to deal with them. They usually arise from below ground-level, but this is not always the case with bushes that have been high planted so that the graft union is above soil-level. Equally, not all shoots rising from below ground-level need be suckers if bushes have been planted with their union below ground-level. Suckers on common bedding roses have smaller and more numerous leaflets than the rose variety, they are plain green, and either have no thorns or more numerous and smaller thorns. As there are several rootstocks in use for the commercial production of roses there is no one single type of sucker to watch for.

Whenever suckers are seen they should be removed; when they are small and young it is easier to do than when they are older and have become woody. Suckers should not be cut

31

off at ground-level because this encourages subterranean buds to grow away and the result is several suckers in place of one. To deal with them effectually first scrape away the soil and expose their point of origin, then take the sucker in a gloved hand and pull sharply downwards; this removes both the sucker and basal buds.

On standards, rub off any shoots which develop along the main stem and remove those that arise from below ground-level.

On species roses that are grafted it can be very difficult to detect suckers for there is a wider range of rootstocks used in their propagation and the suckers from some of these are very similar to the scion variety and difficult to identify. If at all possible, species roses should be purchased on their own roots.

Initial pruning

Bedding roses planted late in the season are pruned at planting time. All roses can be pruned when planting but it is more usual with early plantings to allow them time to establish, pruning in early spring. All shoots are cut hard back: the weaker to two or three buds, the stronger to four or five.

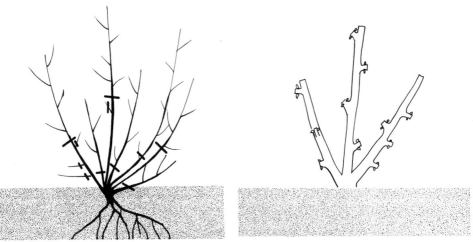

The pruning of shrub or species roses. The first picture shows the unpruned rose, indicating where the cuts should be made, and the second picture shows roses pruned severely.

Standard hybrid teas and floribundas are pruned less severely to seven or eight buds of the union.

Climbing hybrid teas and floribundas are reduced to about half their original length. Too hard pruning of this group can result in their reversion to the bush types of which they are but sports.

Rambler roses are cut to within 9in of the ground, and **weeping standards** to the same distance from the union.

Shrub and species roses are restricted to three main stems, the rest being removed completely. Those remaining are cut to about a third of their original length, all side shoots growing into the bush are removed and the rest cut to within two buds of the main stems.

Pruning of established roses flowering on current season's growth

Roses fall into two groups for pruning purposes: those flowering on current wood and those producing flowers on growth of the previous year. The main sections within the first group are: hybrid teas, floribundas, polyanthas, grandiflora, hybrid perpetuals, hybrid musks, miniatures, china roses and the *rugosa* forms.

Time of pruning The timing of the pruning of this group flowering on current wood has long been controversial, every month from October to May having been recommended. Early spring is still the most popular period because it is claimed that shoots resulting are more likely to escape late frosts. But already at this time sap is rising and growth has begun, so some of the plant's energy will have been wasted, and in some varieties stems bleed following late pruning. Shoots which develop after this pruning are strong and succulent and therefore very susceptible to severe damage should there happen to be any late frosts. By mid-spring, disease organisms are active and likely to invade such damaged tissue.

Autumn pruning has now been generally discontinued. In a mild autumn pruning can force bushes into growth which is killed in the winter. Pruning when the bushes are dormant is undoubtedly the best time, and this is usually January or

February—though in some years growth never seems to cease completely. If, following early pruning, buds do start into growth the shoots develop very slowly and are hardy, acclimatising themselves as they grow and so are better able to withstand damage from late frosts—although they can be damaged by earlier severe weather.

The gardener who has difficulty in making up his mind about when to prune should try bushes at different times and then decide for himself.

Techniques and principles of pruning Bedding roses can flower well and profusely if never pruned, but the framework becomes hard and woody and grows upward with each year. Eventually new growth diminishes, flowers are of poorer quality, the bush is cluttered with dead and dying wood, and disease becomes a problem. Light pruning has a somewhat similar result even if the upward development is slower and

a   b

Pruning a rose. A close-up showing precisely how and where secateurs (pruning shears) should be placed to obtain the correct cut in relation to a bud.

there is no clutter, but flowers, though numerous, will be of poor quality. Hard pruning produces a small bush, well supplied with young growth on which flowers are few but

34

a

b

c

d

Pruning a standard rose. It is worth noting that in addition to shortening back the shoots, weak shoots should be removed altogether.

of the best quality.

As with all pruning, one first carries out the essentials: cutting out all dead and damaged wood and any that shows

35

signs of disease, thinning out crowded branches and removing shoots growing into the centre of the bush. Look at the bush and observe the position, amount and ages of the wood. One-year-old wood is green, two-year-old is brownish-green and wood older than three years is brown or black. From old wood will emerge shoots of one-year, two-year and even older wood, and there will always be a preponderance of older wood at the base of the bush. The aim should be to have a large percentage of one-year-old wood in the bush with most of this coming from, or near, ground-level.

Each year cut out some old wood, removing it to a point where young wood is breaking lower down, or cutting out completely any wood that has no younger wood, or very little, growing from it. At all times the aim should be to get rid of wood older than three years. On two-year-old wood, cut back to the lowest point at which young wood is developing, or if there is only terminal young growth, cut away about a third of the two-year wood. With one-year wood, cut back weak growth to two or three buds and reduce the strong to a half or a third of its original length. Strong-growing varieties should be pruned less severely than weaker ones.

Bush rose prior to pruning. The illustration shows wood of different seasons' growth, thereby indicating how the shape of a rose is built up and retained.

When pruning, make the cut just above the bud horizontally or slightly sloping inwards. Cut always to an outward pointing bud. An exception is made on bushes growing on the outside of a bed when a shoot resulting from an outside bud would be damaged by the mower or perhaps tear the clothes of a passer-by. Stems in such a position can be cut so that the bud develops more or less parallel to the outer edge of the bed.

Small pruning cuts heal readily but larger ones on three-year-old wood need to be sealed. Where a saw has been used, pare the cut surface with a knife before application. After winter pruning apply a spray, combining both insecticide and fungicide to the bushes and the ground beneath.

Pruning removes wood in which food material is stored up and the plant has to make good the growth removed before it can flower. So whenever hard pruning is practised it must go along with applications of organic matter or a dressing of a general rose fertilizer. Beds of roses which have been regularly pruned and fertilized can still be in good healthy condition, flowering well and producing blooms of good quality after sixty years.

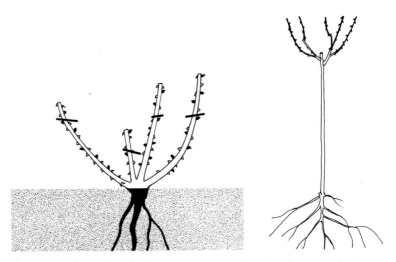

A standard rose as bought from a nurseryman showing the point of union of the graft with the substantially greater root development usually found in standard roses as compared with bush roses.

Following the winter pruning, bushes grow away and by early summer are producing their first flowers. After these have faded, the bushes need to be dead-headed. This improves their appearance and diverts energy which would be used up in the production of fruit into the production of more flowers. Dead-heading does not consist of just removing the dead head but of cutting down to where new growth is emerging, or removing about one-third of the new growth. This is in effect a type of summer pruning which leads on to a good second flush and, if repeated, to a third in some years.

Treatment of neglected roses   After reading so far you may

a

b

Pruning an H.T. rose. The first picture shows the rose newly planted just as it arrived from the nursery. It should then be pruned really hard as shown in the two following pictures. Few people ever prune newly planted roses hard enough.

38   c

Pruning a bush rose prior to planting. The aim is to achieve a balance between top-growth and root growth. The plant in the first picture is completely out of balance, with far too much root in relation to its top-growth. In the final picture a balance has been achieved.

a

b

c

have decided that something ought to be done about those roses which have never been pruned! Can they be brought back into order? Yes, it is possible to get them into good shape again provided that the bushes are not too old. It cannot however be done in one year; you cannot correct long-standing neglect overnight.

Firstly remove all dead, damaged and diseased wood. Open up the centre of the bush, cutting out crossing branches and thinning where crowded; cut back all young wood to within two or three buds of their base. Feed well and apply a combined spray. This should stimulate the bushes into growth and some shoots should be produced low down on the bush.

In the following winter there must be more concentrated effort. Cut out all old wood arising above young shoots produced low down. Remove completely at least one old stem at, or as near as possible to, the ground. Reduce at least one of the older shoots by half and cut back hard all young shoots on the bush. Repeat the entire process the following year, cutting back all the time to where young growth is appearing low down on the bush. It will take at least three years to bring bushes back to normal but each year there should be an improvement in the amount of young wood produced and in the quality of the flowers. If there is no response after two years, the bushes are too old and should be removed.

Pruning of established roses flowering on one-year-old wood

Included in this group are climbing hybrid teas and floribundas, rambler roses, weeping standards, most shrub roses and species. The best time for pruning these is immediately after flowering, but they are often left until the winter,

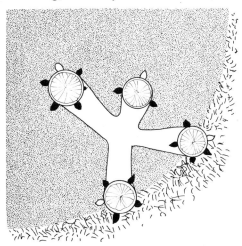

A plan view of a rose-bed showing a pruned rose as seen from above. The buds shown in outline only should be retained in order to produce a well-shaped plant.

especially when they have attractive fruits.

Climbing hybrid teas and floribundas produce new growth from ground-level which should be tipped and tied in. The strongest varieties do this reasonably freely and so all wood which has flowered can be removed completely. Unfortunately most kinds do not refurnish readily and some, perhaps all,

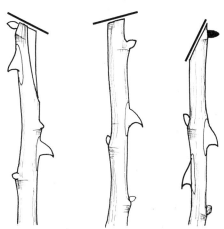

Incorrect pruning cuts. The picture shows on the left, the sort of cut made with a blunt instrument resulting in the tearing or crushing of the wood. The centre illustration shows a cut made too high leaving a snag of wood that will die, probably becoming infected and which could therefore kill the whole plant. The drawing on the right shows a cut made too close to the bud: this will result in the wood dying back to the bud below and presents the same hazards as the cut made too high above the bud.

of their growth which has flowered has to be retained. Along these flowering canes, all the flowering laterals are cut hard back to two buds. The oldest shoots should always be removed whenever enough new shoots have been produced.

Rambler roses grow vigorously and produce an abundance of new shoots annually. All shoots, therefore, which have borne flowers are removed completely. In fact so strong are some varieties that far more stems are produced than are required. Whenever enough shoots have been selected and tied in so as to be well spaced, the remainder should be removed; do not be tempted to keep all just because they are strong and healthy. If these are growing over a tree,

41

however, they can be allowed to grow unpruned except for the removal of dead wood. When climbing over a pergola, old stems are allowed to keep growing to provide a good covering, but all laterals which have flowered are cut hard back. **Weeping standards** are just rambler roses grafted on to a long stem. Following flowering, all stems which have borne flowers are removed completely.

Shrub and species roses can be left unpruned, but without

a   b

attention they become thickets of tangled growth, their centres choked with blind, dead or diseased twigs. Annual pruning is desirable to open up the centre of the bush and thin out crowded shoots. Tipping of young shoots in the winter months helps control mildew to which some kinds, eg *Rosa × alba* are particularly prone.

Roses with long arching branches can be shortened. Some species, eg *R. spinosissima*, have a suckering habit and should have the oldest and weakest stems removed completely. One or two are grown for the winter effect of their stems, eg *R. omiensis pteracantha* which has large red translucent thorns on its young stems. To encourage strong young stems, all are cut to ground-level in early spring.

Rose species which are tender are grown against a wall for protection. *R. banksiae* flowers on sub-laterals of the older

Pruning of a high-grafted weeping rose to produce a longer trunk. The illustrations show the sequence in its 1st, 2nd and 3rd year.

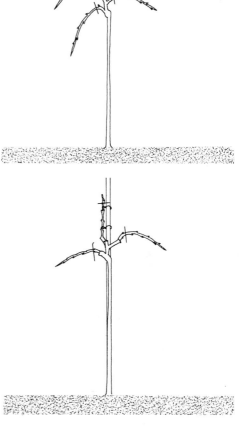

c

Pruning a rambler rose. The first picture shows the unpruned rose at the end of a season's growth. It is then completely removed from its support, laid out on the ground, pruned, and then tied back into position.

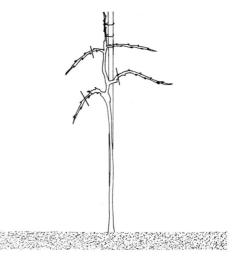

wood and sometimes on wood produced the previous year; after training in a well-spaced framework, it does not need a great deal of pruning. Following flowering the surplus long shoots coming away from the wall are cut back, thinning takes place and the rest are tied in when some of the older wood is removed.

Climbing roses showing how the canes that have flowered should be cut out leaving the new canes. The example shown here is a rambler rose.

R. bracteata and its hybrid 'Mermaid' have pithy stems which are readily damaged by extreme cold, especially when wood fails to ripen properly after a wet summer. The young stems are very brittle and easily snapped off so care must be exercised when tying in. Carry out pruning in spring, removing any winter-damaged wood, cutting back shoots which have flowered and thinning generally. When growing well, large amounts of shoots are produced and in a wet summer an end-of-summer thinning of non-flowering shoots will aid the ripening of wood.

Special types of pruning

Hedges Some of the more vigorous bushy kinds of roses can be used to make low hedges up to about 6ft in height. These are informal, producing flowers, and so are trimmed rather than clipped to strict formality. Amongst suitable floribundas are the old variety 'Frensham' or the newer 'Queen Elizabeth'; many shrub roses make good hedges, eg the hybrid musks and 'Nevada'; and of the many species suitable are *R. rugosa* and its hybrids and *R. rubiginosa* and its hybrid group, the 'Penzance Briars'.

Plant in well-prepared ground at 3–4ft intervals and cut hard back to about 9in to produce strong growth from ground-level. In the following winter, remove about half of the new wood, and so on each year until the hedge has reached its maximum height. Hedges flowering on current season's growth are trimmed to shape in winter and any dead wood removed. When flowers are from the previous year's growth trim after flowering.

Newly planted H.T. rose, showing just how severely these should be pruned. Weak shoots should be pruned right back to buds and stronger shoots back to five buds. Very few people even prune newly-planted roses hard enough.

45

Rosa 'China Town' trained as a tie-down rose. The main shoots are bent over and secured to the framework of wires.

5
Tools and Equipment

Tools used for pruning are numerous and varied and each has been devised for a specific purpose. There are three groups: knives, secateurs (pruning shears) and saws (*see* Chapter 12 for hedge trimming tools).

Knives

Today the use of knives is limited because few people know how to use them properly, but in the hands of a skilled operator they are still the best pruning tool. There are a number on the market, of differing sizes and patterns, which are sold as pruning knives, but in fact almost any kind of knife can be used for pruning provided the blade is of good steel, capable of keeping a good edge, and is firmly set into the handle so that it cannot come loose under pressure.

A pruning knife must be sharp; a blunt knife is useless and can also be dangerous. More wounds are inflicted with blunt knives than with sharp ones, because more pressure has to be applied to make them cut and this is when they are likely to slip. When pruning, hold the branch below the point where the cut is to be made. Start with the knife behind the branch, just below the level of the chosen bud. With a slightly upward movement make the cut at an angle, to finish just above the bud.

A knife should be sharpened on an oil-stone. Inspection of the blade will indicate how it was sharpened in the factory:

often one side of the blade is flat and the other has been sharpened at an angle, sometimes both have been sharpened at an angle. Where possible, sharpen to the same angle as previously. However, some people find it difficult to keep a knife blade at a fixed angle, and they may have to compromise and sharpen both sides flat on the stone.

Keep your pruning knife for just this task. Don't use it for cutting any old thing or for prizing tacks out of wood or the edge of the blade will soon become chipped—even with constant care this can too easily happen. If the blade does become chipped, grind the edge down until it is again straight and then sharpen in the normal manner. Once a blade has been sharpened a keen edge can be produced and maintained as necessary by rubbing on a razor strop.

Though knives may not be in regular use for pruning there are some jobs for which they have to be used: paring smooth the rind after sawing off a branch; gouging out diseased material from a branch prior to painting with a wound protectant; trimming back young growth that has been damaged by late frosts; and removing twiggy growths along trunks so as not to leave basal buds. After use the blade should always be wiped clean and any matter adhering removed by emery paper. Rub the blade with an oily cloth and put a drop of oil on the pivot to make for easier movement.

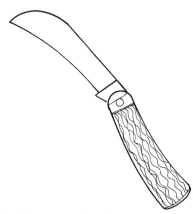

A pruning knife. There is a definite art to using these knives and any competent rose nurseryman will demonstrate it to you. If you can master the art it will give a good, clean cut.

Secateurs (Pruning Shears)

Secateurs carry out the work that was formerly done with the pruning knife. Their use requires little effort and no special skill; they are an indispensable aid to the gardener. There are two main types: the parrot beak with two cutting blades, and the anvil with one.

Parrot-beak type These are so called because of the shape of the cutting blades. They are available in several sizes, the products of different manufacturers varying slightly in design and size range. One type has a swivel handle which takes wrist fatigue out of the job. These are used in one hand and are capable of cutting stems of up to half an inch easily and up to three-quarters of an inch with care. Do not try to cut heavier wood with them. When cutting use a straight action and avoid twisting the blades.

After use, remove ingrained dirt with emery paper and before putting away wipe all parts with an oily cloth and put a spot of oil on the pivot and spring. When not actually working with them keep the catch on and the blades together. Most manufacturers or their agents will service their tools for a small fee, and if these are in regular use annual attention is desirable.

Anvil type These have an anvil which holds the stem

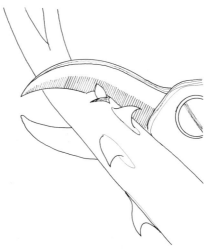

Parrot-beak secateurs in action.

49

while the single blade does the cutting. They are available in several sizes and with one or two special modifications, eg for cutting wire. They need a little more attention in handling than the previous type. Make the blade do the cutting; do not try to make the anvil push the stem against the cutting edge. Always have the blade where it can be seen and place the blade above the bud when making the cut. Again, do not attempt to cut wood that is too thick; like the parrot-beak type, these will easily cope with wood up to half an inch, and with care up to three-quarters. Avoid twisting the blades when cutting as this strains them and causes the

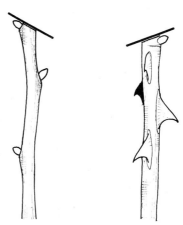

The correct angle of pruning. The cut should always be made so that it slopes slightly back and away from the bud at which it is made.

blade to cut off centre, which results in bruising or tearing of the bark. The blade must be sharp at all times and the anvil in good condition. After continued use the blade can cause a groove along the anvil or ingrained dirt may accumulate to provide an uneven surface and inefficient cutting with bruising and tearing will certainly follow. Sending your pruning shears or secateurs away annually for service ensures that they remain in good condition.

When a pruning job is finished see that all ingrained dirt, either on the blade or the anvil, is removed with emery paper and all metal parts are rubbed with an oily cloth. A drop of oil should be introduced into the pivot. Fasten when not in use

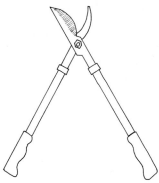

Long-handled pruners, also known as stumpers or loppers. The extra length of the handles gives one considerable cutting power, and these are designed to be used to cut hard, old wood.

so that the blade is kept against the anvil.

Long-handled secateurs or loppers   These are modifications of the anvil or parrot-beak type on handles about 18in long. The blade or blades open wider, and as with the longer handles there is more leverage the loppers can cope easily with wood up to three-quarters of an inch and with care up to one inch, their longer handles give a greater reach. Two hands

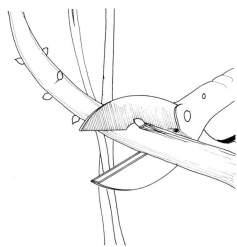

Anvil-type secateurs in action. The cut should be made with the blade on top of the bud so that the actual position of the cut can be seen.

are needed to operate them.

Long-arms or long-armed pruners These are anvil-type secateurs fixed on the end of a pole which comes in varying lengths up to 9ft. The single cutting blade is operated by a wire attached to a handle. When the handle is in the up position the blade is open; to operate, pull down the handle and this drives the blade on to its anvil. This high-reaching tool also needs two hands, one to hold and one to operate.

Saws

Joiner's or carpenter's saws can be used for pruning, but saws manufactured for the job are to be preferred for they stand up better to the rougher work and are easier to insert and use in difficult places. Saws take over from secateurs when branches of more than 1-in thickness have to be cut.

Narrow-bladed saw This type has one cutting edge, is between half an inch and an inch in width, and has a folding handle. It can deal with wood up to one and a half inches in diameter but above this the work becomes tiring. Its main use is to saw awkwardly placed small branches or to remove one branch where several are growing close together and loppers cannot be used.

Pruning saw This is two-edged, with larger teeth on one side than on the other. It is used for branches up to perhaps 3in diameter, the initial rougher work being carried out with the larger teeth and the final finishing cut made with the smaller. The one trouble with this type of saw is that it is unsuitable for dealing with branches growing close together, as damage can be caused by the second cutting edge. After use, remove sawdust from the teeth with a wire brush and wipe with an oily rag. Send away regularly for sharpening.

Grecian saw The curved blade has teeth along one side only. It can be used for the same tasks as the pruning saw and is preferable to it.

Bow saw Here we have a metal frame with a detachable saw blade which is capable of dealing with all branches as long as there is enough space to operate; replace with a new blade when the old one shows signs of wear.

When sawing off a small branch, take its weight so that it does not break away and tear the bark. If one does not have a

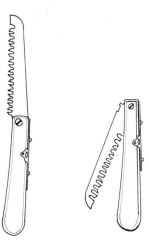

Narrow-bladed pruning saw. These folding types are particularly useful.

free hand or if the branch is large, it should first be undercut until the wood begins to pinch; then remove the saw and start on the top of the branch. Don't worry about being directly above the lower cut. This does not matter. As the branch parts from the tree it will break cleanly between the two cuts. The stub remaining should then be cut off neatly, finishing just slightly proud of the trunk.

A large limb should be removed in pieces. When in the centre of the tree or high in the crown, large branches or parts to be cut away should be roped to higher branches so they do not fall and damage wood below.

Ladders and steps

When pruning has to be carried out on trees and even on some large shrubs, some if not all of the branches may be out of reach and a ladder or steps will be necessary. Ensure that these are in good condition and securely placed.

Sealing applications

The removal of any part of a plant causes a wound which has to heal. Just below the bark of a shrub or tree is a single, continuous layer of cells known as the cambium. Following a

53

a   b

Removing a double leader. If a double leader is allowed to develop, sooner or later the crutch will collect water, rot and the tree literally split itself down the middle.

cut, these cells begin to divide, producing callus tissue which forms in a ring around the circumference of the cut and continues to increase inwards for varying distances, depending on the size of cut, age, vigour, condition and kind of tree or shrub. On small young branches, the entire end of the cut may be sealed in this way, but on thicker and older wood healing may not be complete and callus may only form around the edge of the cut.

Roughly cut, broken, torn or bruised wood is slow to heal because the ring of cambium has been broken and a complete seal is rarely possible. Broken branches or those roughly cut with a large-toothed saw, should have the stubs taken off with a finer-toothed saw and the edge of the bark pared smooth with a sharp knife. Where tears have taken place, all the edges of exposed bark should be pared smooth.

The formation of callus tissue prevents the entry of disease organisms and so it is important that this healing process should be as rapid as possible. It is quite fast on young shoots but it can take a long time where old and large branches have been removed. All cuts above an inch should be treated with a wound dressing which provides a protection against disease entry until the healing process is complete.

For those trees that are slow to heal, especially in winter months (eg magnolias), pruning may be more suitably done in late summer when callus tissue forms more quickly.

6
Alphabetical List of Genera

Alphabetical list of genera with some additional species

Abbreviations:
D Deciduous	T Tree
E Evergreen	C Conifer
L Leafless	Cl Climber
S Shrub	× Hybrid origin

Abelia DS Most species are tender and need a sheltered position or wall. In the spring, remove winter damage, thin crowded shoots and remove some old wood.

Abeliophyllum DS A shrub with a sprawling habit, usually grown against a wall to give protection to its early flowers. After flowering, cut out shoots on which flowers have been produced. If grown as a free-standing shrub, rather harder pruning is necessary following flowering to correct the sprawling habit.

Abies (fir) **EC** Select a single leader and retain all side branches.

Abutilon DS All species are tender and usually grown as wall shrubs. In May cut out winter damage and thin out crowded shoots. **Abutilon vitifolium** should be treated as a free-standing shrub and succeeds best where there is some summer humidity; the only pruning needed is dead-heading.

Acer (maple) DS/T   A large family of varying habits, size and attractions all of which have to be considered when pruning.

Trees are trained to a central leader. If the leader is lost a new one must be trained in or the opposite buds will result in two leaders; in some species it is difficult to retain a leader. Carry out pruning when fully dormant, some species bleed if cut when the sap is rising. Bushes may be allowed to have several leaders though often a central one is trained in but with all side shoots retained.

Coloured leaf forms of *A. negundo* should never be pruned hard otherwise the resulting shoots revert to green. Training in the early days should consist of little more than pinching. Those trees grown for their bark should have their trunks exposed as soon as possible; an annual trimming of the previous year's growth on the snake bark maples will result in long, colourful young stems. All species are likely to suffer damage from the fungus known as coral spot. This initially infects dead wood but spreads to the living, killing stems and even branches; if it girdles a young tree, death can result.

Actinidia DC1   Slightly tender, vigorous twiners that need plenty of space. Once a well-spaced framework has been achieved by training in several long stems opposite and parallel, young stems are cut back in April to within two or three buds of this framework; repeat the process in July so as to build up a spur system.

Akebia DC1   Strong climbers which need plenty of space and which will become an unmanageable tangle unless regular pruning is practised. In June cut out all shoots which have flowered and thin drastically any remaining. If pruning has been neglected, shear off at about 3ft from the ground, retrain a framework and start again.

Amelanchier DS/T   For pruning purposes, there are two types: one suckers and remains a shrub, the other becomes tree-like. The first is pruned in January when the oldest stems are removed; the second, a central leader is trained, all

56

side shoots being reduced but retained as long as possible.

Ampelopsis DC1   All are strong growers and need plenty of space. They are well suited for growing through a tree where no pruning is required. If space is restricted train in a number of rods (mature shoots) and in January cut back all young shoots to within two or three buds of the rods. Bleeding will follow if pruning is delayed until the sap begins to rise.

Aralia DS   Stems arising from a rootstock are stout and pithy and liable to be damaged in winter if they do not ripen properly. The chief attraction is the large compound leaves of which there are variegated forms. Retain only a few stems and remove the rest at ground-level each spring.

Aronia (chokeberry) DS   If grown for flowers and fruit as well as autumn colour, thin out only the crowded branches during winter. If grown only for autumn colour, reduce all shoots by half.

Artemisia ES   A few species are woody and these are somewhat tender. Remove winter damage in May and trim to shape. As these plants are grown for their foliage, flower spikes can be removed as they form.

Atriplex ES   Some species are tender. All kinds tend to sprawl, especially if grown in shade or a rich soil. Trim moderately hard in April to correct this habit.

Aucuba ES   Trim to shape in April, occasionally cutting out some of the oldest wood. This shrub will respond to hard pruning if it becomes too large.

Azalea *see* **Rhododendron**

Bamboos ES   (The different genera are all included under this heading for their pruning is identical.) Cut out discoloured stems, dead and thin stems, as well as those which have flowered in April. The bamboos which spread by underground runner can be invasive and some means of confining them may be necessary. Once flowering begins death follows, not always immediately but each year thereafter the clumps decline.

Berberis D/ES   Some evergreen kinds are tender and need shelter. All evergreen berberries should be pruned after flowering, but if berries are wanted delay until the following April when those shoots having borne fruit are removed. Most deciduous kind form dense thickets and these should be thinned in July, removing completely at ground-level. If old bushes become unmanageable they can be cut down to ground-level after flowering.

Buddleia D/ES   Many species are tender and need a south or west wall for protection; these are trained fan-wise, ensuring that the lowest part of the wall is kept clothed.

Buddleias which flower on current season's growth, eg *B. davidii*, are cut hard back to a framework in the winter; tender species are similarly treated in April. Buddleias which flower on the previous year's growth, eg *B. globosa*, are pruned following flowering when the shoots which have carried flowers are removed. *Buddleia alternifolia* is best treated as a standard. Select the strongest shoots, removing the others, and tie to a stake; continue feathering until there is a clear stem of at least 4ft after which natural development can be allowed.

Buxus ES/T   If of tree form, select a single leader, removing competition; side shoots are reduced but retained as long as possible except if too crowded. The bush kinds, of which there are many different forms, should be trimmed to shape in April when some corrective pruning may be necessary, especially if heavy snow has caused any damage.

Callicarpa DS   All species are tender to some degree. Prune in April cutting out any winter damage and thinning out crowded shoots.

Calluna (ling) ES   Trim over the clumps in March, removing old flowers and most of last year's growth. The dwarf forms such as 'Foxii' and 'Foxii Nana' are not pruned at all except to remove dead wood. Plants grown just for foliage are often best trimmed as the flower spikes form for the colours of flower and foliage often clash.

Camellia ES   Some species are tender and need wall protection. *C. japonica* and its many forms are hardy though often flower-bud tender. Dead-heading is desirable on those kinds which do not shed their spent flowers; at the same time trim to shape or restrict growth.

Camellia japonica sports freely and several colours can appear amongst flowers on one bush. Branches bearing different-coloured flowers should be traced to their source and removed. *Camellia sasanqua* and *C. cuspidata* are autumn-flowering species and if pruning is necessary carry this out in April.

Tender species and some of the forms of *C. japonica* may be grown as wall shrubs. Fan train a well-spaced framework and allow side branches to develop just sufficiently to fill the intervening spaces, remove surplus shoots as well as any coming away from the wall.

Campsis DC1   These slightly tender climbers need full sun and a south wall. They are strong growers, attaching themselves to supports by climbing roots. Once a well-spaced framework has been trained with the lower part of the wall well-clothed, all side shoots should be cut back in early spring to within two or three buds.

Caryopteris DS   Unless the wood is thoroughly ripened, die-back is common. In April cut back all young shoots to a framework which is best trained on a short leg.

Ceanothus D/ES   All evergreens are tender and the decidous kinds reasonably hardy.

The evergreen kinds can be, and are often, grown against a wall. Plant from containers and ensure that plants are not root-bound. It is usual to train a parallel framework to cover the wall, ensuring as always that the lower parts are kept clothed. Prune after flowering, cutting only the young growth hard back to the framework. If treated as free-standing shrubs, they are trained to several leaders and trimmed each year, following flowering, back to this framework; winter damage is removed and some thinning may be desirable. Avoid cutting into old wood as this is slow to break.

The deciduous kinds flower on current season's growth which is cut down to ground-level or to a framework in April.

Ceratostigma ES All species are somewhat tender, but though they may be cut back to ground-level in a cold winter they usually break away freely so long as the roots are undamaged. Flowering is on current season's growth and all growth surviving the winter is cut back to ground-level in April.

Cercis DT It is not easy to train and retain a single leader but this is the best method. Reduce side shoots and gradually remove them. *Cercis* is generally grown as a shrub, with little pruning. It is, however, important to train in a satisfactory framework and give a light trimming after flowering to remove the immature seed pods. The production of these can be excessive and if left will reduce vigour and extension growth.

Chaenomeles (Japanese quince) DS There are spur-bearing shrubs and once regular flowering begins, little pruning is required. Select several leaders and train to a well-balanced framework. An encouragement to help in producing spurs is to cut back all side shoots to three or four buds in the winter months. It is important to keep the centre of the bush open and any shoots intruding should be removed.

If grown as wall shrubs to gain some protection for the precocious flowers, they are trained fan-wise. All side shoots are then shortened and after the spur system has formed no further pruning should be required.

Chamaecyparis (false cypress) EC There are many species and a great number of cultivars of varying sizes, shapes and colour; no attempt to prune to shape should be made. Many of these cvs produce several leaders, which can easily be over-

60

looked when the tree is young for then they in no way spoil the shape and are usually hidden by foliage. In their early years these are no trouble, but with age the leaders fall away and spoil the outline; surreptitious wiring is necessary to pull them together. The dwarf and small-growing kinds need no pruning.

Chimonanthus (winter sweet) DS   Although fully hardy this shrub does not flower freely unless the wood is properly ripened. For this reason, and to obtain some protection for its flowers during the winter, it is usually grown against a wall. Trained fan-wise, the framework is tied to supports, and all branches coming away from the wall are removed. In July all side branches are cut back to two or three buds of the main framework. In a wet summer any excess growth should be thinned at the end of August to encourage better ripening.

Free-standing shrubs are trained to several leaders and all side shoots are shortened back to two or three buds in July.

Choisya (Mexican orange) ES   This shrub may be damaged in a colder-than-average winter, so plant in a position protected from cold winds. Dead-head following pruning, trimming to shape at the same time.

Cistus ES   All species are tender to some extent, needing full sun and a well-drained, not too rich soil. Following flowering, remove dead flowers and their stems as well as any winter damage and trim to shape.

Clematis D/EC1   If space permits, these climbers can be left to their own devices with a minimum of pruning; most of the species are treated in this way.

They fall more or less into two groups. Those flowering on current season's growth, eg the *jackmanii*, *lanuginosa* and *viticella* groups. These can be cut down to ground-level in February. To extend the flowering season, some stems can be left unpruned either in their entirety or reduced in length. These shoots should be removed completely in the following year.

The second group flowers on short growth from stems produced in the previous year. Included here are the *patens*,

61

florida and *montana* groups. These are pruned after flowering, when shoots which have carried flowers are removed and there is a thinning of excess growth. The *florida* and *patens* groups sometimes produce a late flush of flowers and such shoots are reduced following flowering.

One or two species such as *C. recta* and *C. heracleaefolia* are non-climbers; the former is usually cut to ground-level each February whilst the second is cut back to a framework.

Clethra D/ES   The deciduous species are hardier than the evergreen and have a suckering habit; there should be a thinning out of shoots at ground-level in March. The evergreen group need a favoured position to succeed and are usually trained to a single leader but all side shoots are retained.

Cornus DS/T   For pruning purposes this genus can be divided into those that sucker and those that develop a single stem. The former tend to make clumps and these should be thinned out during the winter when all shoots which have carried fruit can be removed. A number of these shrubs have attractively coloured stems which are cut to ground-level annually in March.

A single leader should be selected for the kinds which become trees; side shoots should be reduced but retained as long as possible.

Coronilla ES   Some species are tender and need protection. Prune in April, trimming back shoots to about half their length.

Corylopsis DS   Flowers are produced during the winter on one-year-old wood. No pruning is necessary unless one wishes to restrict growth, in which case prune after flowering.

Corylus DS/T   A few species are tree-like and these are trained to a central leader. Suckering along the trunk is common and these should be rubbed off whilst still soft in May. Mostly the species are shrub-like with a strong tendency to sucker; these are trimmed after flowering to restrict them,

62

and the suckers are also removed. *C. avellana*, the hazel, and *C. maxima* the filbert or cob, are grown in coppices for their nuts, and *C. avellana* may be cut down to ground-level every few years for brushwood. Both the hazel and cobnut are grown in gardens for their winter catkins; some trimming is needed following flowering. Both have purple-leaved forms which are pruned quite hard after flowering.

Cotinus (smokebush) ES   *C. coggygria* and *cotinoides* may still be better known under their classification of *Rhus*. If grown for their smoky flowers there is little pruning except to thin out crowded shoots and to tip shoots in the winter months. When growing the purple-leaved forms of either species for autumn colour, hard pruning in the winter months can be practised.

Cotoneasters E/DS/T   The strongest-growing kinds such as *C. frigida* can be trained to a single leader to form trees. There are one or two pendulous forms such as *C. salicifolia* which can be trained as weeping standards. A single leader is trained up a stake and all side shoots pinched back until there is a clear 6ft stem. Sometimes they are high grafted on to a 6ft stem. Cut back all side shoots in April and train in a well-spaced framework.

Cotoneasters grown as shrubs only require thinning and restriction of growth; evergreens are pruned in April and the deciduous kinds in winter. The prostrate forms which are used as ground cover benefit from an occasional thinning to let in the light. One or two species such as *C. horizontalis*, lend themselves to training against an east- or north-facing wall. Form a well-spaced framework, removing any branches which come away from the wall and thinning out the young branches without destroying the grace of the natural habit.

Fireblight is a troublesome disease with this genus.

Crataegus (thorns) DS/T   Almost all kinds will form small trees if trained to a single leader; they are, being small in stature, well suited to training as standards. Following training, the only pruning necessary is to remove crossing branches and to carry out thinning during the winter months.

Those to be trained as shrubs can have three leaders. Subsequent pruning consists of keeping the centre of the bush open and carrying out judicious thinning in March.

This genus is susceptible to fireblight disease, the symptoms of which are most obvious in June.

Cupressocyparis leylandii EC   This hybrid is fast growing, well anchored and is much planted in exposed conditions for windbreaks. Plant shrubs from open ground rather than from containers. Select and retain a single leader.

Cupressus (cypress) EC   Most species are tender. Select and retain a single leader, shortening back the side branches on the kinds that spread. In general no trimming is necessary and all side shoots should be retained as long as possible.

Cydonia (quince) DS   Suckers are freely produced so it is better to train the framework on a short leg. Flowering is on spurs and once established no pruning is necessary, but in the early years side shoots can be shortened back to two or three buds from the framework. Ensure that the centre of the bush is kept open.

Cytisus (broom) DS   Prune after flowering, cutting back to where new shoots are breaking. Avoid cutting into old wood. At the same time cut out crowded shoots and open up the centre of the bush.

C. battandieri is so different from other brooms that one may be excused for thinking it a different genus. It is slightly tender and often grown against a wall. Either as a wall shrub or free standing, it needs little pruning except for cutting out winter damage in April. Thin and cut out some of the old wood occasionally.

Daboecia (St Daboec's heath) ES   Shear over the bushes in April, taking off old flower stalks and most of the last year's growth; to shape at the same time.

Daphne E/DS   In general these shrubs are left unpruned. *D. mezereum* is an exception for if left unpruned it becomes

64

gaunt with long bare stems. Each spring remove those twigs which have carried the flowers. If the prostrate kinds develop long bare stems, these should be pegged down and covered with soil: they will root and in time, form dense clumps.

Deutzia DS Pruning follows flowering, when the shoots which have carried flowers are removed. Open up the centre of the bush and cut out shoots that are crowded.

D. scabra is a strong upright grower and has the added attraction of an interesting bark. Leave unpruned, carrying out judicious thinning only.

Diervilla DS Following flowering, cut back to where new growth is breaking and thin.

Elaeagnus (oleaster) **D/ES/T** The strongest growers can be trained as small trees by selecting a single leader. Later pruning is to thin and trim. The less vigorous growers are allowed several leaders and trained as shrubs. Most are grown for their foliage and all benefit from annual pruning. Deciduous kinds should have side shoots cut hard back in March and the centres of the bush kept open. Evergreens should be pruned in April when they may be thinned and trimmed to shape. As some of the variegated forms have a tendency to revert any plain green shoots should be removed at their point of origin.

Embothrium (Chilean firebush) **DS/T** These shrubs and trees are sensitive to soil and atmospheric conditions and if these are unfavourable growth will be unsatisfactory. Pruning is undesirable, and confined to correcting mis-shapen branches after flowering.

Enkianthus DS Carry out dead-heading, thinning at the same time.

Erica (heath) **ES** Only the European species are commonly grown in gardens and one or two of these are tender. Annual pruning is necessary to keep the clumps tidy, compact and floriferous. Using shears, remove old flowers and most of the

65

previous year's growth; the winter and spring flowers should be clipped after flowering and the summer and autumn flowers in February. Those with coloured foliage can be cut again as the flowers form, for flower and foliage colour do not always blend.

Escallonia ES Whilst generally considered to be tender, most, especially the hybrids, will survive all but the coldest winters. Flowering is on current season's growth and once a framework has been formed, prune hard to within two or three buds of this. In cold districts and for the definitely tender species wall cultivation is necessary. After training a well-spaced fan of branches, cut back all laterals hard in May.

Eucalyptus ET Only a few species of this large family are sufficiently hardy for cultivation in this country. Failure is most often due to poor siting and planting of specimens that are too large and root-bound. Plant small container-grown specimens in an open site but protected from cold winds. A mass of shoots will be produced on the sapling, but eventually one will develop more strongly to become a leader whilst the remaining side shoots will die away. Later, branches are shed to leave a clean bole.

Eucalyptus has two stages of growth, juvenile and adult; the shape and colour of leaves at each stage may be quite different. Foliage is much in demand by the floral arranger, the juvenile foliage usually being the more popular. Cutting of foliage can take place at any time of the year except when in active growth, but excessive cutting should be avoided during the winter months. When adult shoots are cut the new ones arising will be juvenile and a tree can be kept in this state indefinitely by regular hard pruning in early May.

Euonymus (spindle tree) D/ES/T A few species will make trees and these are kept to a single leader, the side branches being shortened and gradually removed. The shrubby kinds are allowed several leaders and in general little pruning is necessary except to thin, trim and keep the centres of the bush open.

The deciduous kinds are sometimes grown primarily for

66

their autumn colour and these can be pruned more severely to encourage strong young growth; this is carried out in March. The best known evergreen is *E. japonicus*, of which there are many variegated forms, some of them very prone to reversion. This species, which is grown mainly for its foliage, is trimmed to shape at the same time as the other evergreens are pruned, in April. This species is very prone to attacks by mildew which can become so bad that normal spraying gives little control. If this happens, severe pruning will remove the unsightly foliage, and the new growth, it is to be hoped, will stay clean.

Euphorbia ES   Whilst most of this genus is herbaceous, a number are woody. These produce upright, rather succulent stems copiously from a rootstock. After flowering cut out at ground-level all shoots which have flowered and all weak stems. When growth is not strong carry out dead-heading, cutting out completely some of the oldest stems.

Exochorda DS   These have a suckering habit and are best trained on a short leg before branching is permitted. Pruning, when necessary, should follow flowering; thin crowded shoots and trim to shape.

× **Fatshedera lizei** (fatheaded Lizzy) ES   This hybrid has a rather sprawling habit and may be trained up a north or east wall or used as ground cover. Pruning is rarely necessary.

Fatsia ES   Remove dead leaves in April and cut out any bare gaunt shoots at ground-level.

Forsythia DS   Hard pruning encourages growth at the expense of flowering so annual pruning should be no more than the removal of crowded shoots from the centre of the bush and a proportion of the oldest wood. When pruning an old or an extra large shrub spread the operation over three years; begin by removing the oldest wood and, as new growth is produced, this can be tipped in early summer.

F. suspensa is often grown against a wall where its long pendulous shoots are displayed to better advantage. A

67

well-spaced fan-shaped framework is trained and tied and from this develop the long weeping branched stems. These are cut hard back to the framework following flowering. When desired as free-standing shrubs, several are planted together so as to give each other support. After planting, reduce the shoots by half or even more; the following winter cut back to where they begin to curve over. Once a rigid framework has been formed shoots can be allowed to develop freely; subsequent pruning is to remove some or all of the shoots which have flowered.

Fuchsia DS   Only a few species are hardy enough for cultivation out of doors all the year round and even those can be cut down in a cold winter but the bushes usually break away freely from ground-level. In May prune back all one-year shoots almost to ground-level or to a framework.

Garrya (tassel bush) ES   Male and female flowers are produced on different plants and it is the male kind with the long catkins that is grown in gardens. Pruning consists of thinning and trimming to shape in April.

Although hardy if given protection against cold winds, is frequently planted against a wall where there is some protection for the winter catkins which then grow longer. After training in a well-spaced framework, some trimming should be carried out in April.

Gaultheria ES   Many species are small growing or prostrate and need almost no pruning. Even the taller kinds require little attention beyond cutting out some of the oldest wood and trimming to shape in April. *G. shallon* is often used as game or ground cover and if it becomes untidy it can be cut hard in April.

Genista LS   Pruning is generally unnecessary except to deadhead and trim to shape at the same time.

Griselinia littoralis (broadwood) ES   Generally considered to be hardy except in the coldest districts, although there does seem to be a variation in hardiness amongst different forms. Trim to shape in April.

68

Halesia DS   Strong growers that will make trees if restricted to a central leader, when feathering will be beneficial. Annual pruning is minimal and consists of removing crossing branches and keeping the centres of bushes open.

Hamamelis (witch hazel) DS   Pruning is generally unnecessary. Most kinds offered for sale are grafted, so watch for suckers; as these closely resemble the desired plant remove all shoots coming from below ground-level.

H. japonica arborea will make a small tree if trained to a single leader; shorten the lower shoots but leave them as long as possible.

Hebe ES   A large genus from New Zealand, of varying hardiness, size and form, often as important for foliage as for flower. A number are tender and should be planted at the foot of a wall. Those that flower early in the year, eg *H. hulkeana*, are pruned after flowering when all shoots which have carried flowers are cut out and there is some trimming. Autumn-flowerers are pruned in May when shortening of the shoots is practised and some thinning.

The hardy kinds need little attention except a trimming to shape in April.

Hedera (ivy) EC1   Ivy comes to mind at once when it is a matter of trying to decide on a climber for a wall. It can, however, be invasive and if left unattended can dislodge slates and gutters.

Ivy has two stages of growth: the juvenile with angular leaves and climbing roots, and the later stage when side branches without roots are produced, leaves become rounder and flowering takes place. It can be slow to start growing up a wall. Train a well-balanced framework, paying attention to clothing, especially at the base of the wall. Cut well back from windows, doors, pipes, gutters and the roof. When branching starts, these should be cut hard back to the wall in April; it is only the young shoots with roots that stick themselves to the wall and once these die there is no hold. Each year cut out some of the oldest wood so that the ivy cover does not with age become so heavy that it falls away from the wall.

69

Controversy has long ranged as to whether ivy growing up a tree is harmful to it. As long as the tree is in good health no damage is done.

Hibiscus DS   Mainly a tropical genus; only one of the species, *H. syriacus*, is commonly seen in modern gardens. This flowers on current season's growth, and once a framework has been trained all young shoots are cut back to within a few buds of it in spring. Coral spot can be troublesome, especially when the shrub is not growing well.

Hippophae (sea buckthorn) DS/T   Male and female flowers are born on separate bushes and so to obtain berries they are often planted in groups with one male to four or five females. Though most often grown as shrubs, they make small trees if trained to a single leader with the lower side shoots reduced. Little pruning is required except to trim and thin during the dormant season.

Hydrangea E/DS/Cl   Hydrangeas often take a year or two to settle down before they start to flower regularly. In general they are little pruned except to dead-head and thin out growth in April.

Climbing hydrangeas attach themselves to their support by means of roots, and as with ivy there are two stages— juvenile growth which clings tight to its support and, when the support has been covered, branching growth with the production of flowers. These flowering shoots are cut back hard in April.

H. macrophylla, the common hydrangea, flowers on one-year wood and pruning consists of the removal of all, or part of the shoot which has flowered and the cutting out of weak shoots. In wet seasons a more drastic thinning may be necessary to help ripen the wood. The old flower heads are often of interest throughout the winter, and as in cold districts, they give protection to overwintering flowerbuds pruning can be delayed until April. A few kinds, eg *H. paniculata*, flower on current season's growth and these are cut hard back to a framework or to ground-level during March.

Hypericum (St John's wort) DS   A few species are tender.

70

Flowers are produced on current season's growth and in April all shoots are cut to within a few inches of the ground. Larger plants can be produced by thinning and tipping the young growth.

Ilex (holly) E/DS/T Hollies are often slow to establish but having done so, grow away strongly. The strong growers which are to become trees should have a single leader selected but all side shoots retained until they die naturally. Pruning consists of trimming to shape in spring. Neglected hollies or those disfigured by leaf miner can be cut back in spring or in summer. It is preferable to carry out this operation over two or three years rather than all at once.

Jasminum E/DCl/S Some species are tender and need protection. Both the climbers and free-standing shrubs need little pruning except to remove some of the wood which has flowered. This can be carried out after flowering with most, but for those that flower over a long period pruning should be done in spring. *J. nudiflorum* should be pruned after flowering, removing most of the wood that has flowered. This increases flowering and keeps the climber tidier.

Juniperus (juniper) EC Some forms make trees and these should be trained to a central leader, with all side shoots retained. The bushes can have several leaders but in spring the centres should be cleared of the clutter of shoots, dead and alive. Dwarf and prostrate junipers are not pruned.

Kalmia ES Very little pruning except for dead-heading. When bushes become straggly or there is an excess of old wood, hard pruning can be practised during spring.

Kerria DS Flowers are produced on the previous year's growth of bright green stems, so attractive in winter. Kerria has a suckering habit, forming large clumps which may need to be restricted. Cut out old canes at ground-level as flowers fade.

Kolkwitzia (beauty bush) DS This bush can be left to develop

71

Pruning evergreens. Most evergreens should be pruned in May. Care should be taken not to cut the leaves, as they will brown where cut.

naturally except for the thinning of shoots where crowded. If space is limited, annual pruning can be done in midsummer when shoots which have flowered are cut out.

Laburnocytisus DT× Some of the flowers are pink, but yellow laburnum flowers and purple broom flowers also appear on the same tree. At flowering time cut away some of the shoots bearing yellow flowers for these grow away at the expense of those with pink flowers which will decline unless given this assistance.

Laburnum (golden chain) DT Most commonly grown as small trees and often trained as standards, for which they are well suited, although a single leader is to be preferred. Strong vertical shoots tend to appear from low down on the tree and these should be removed as they appear.

Laburnum responds well to spur pruning so that trees can be restricted in size by cutting back side shoots to two or three buds in the winter; they are well suited to pleaching. The trees seed heavily and the immature seed pods should be removed, especially as the seed is poisonous.

Laurus (bay) ES/T Slightly tender and susceptible to damage from low temperatures or exposure to cold winds. Train to a central leader, retaining all side branches as long as possible. Bays are commonly seen trimmed, an operation which is carried out in April.

Lavandula (lavender) ES A few species are tender and need the base of a warm south wall. These are trimmed to shape in the spring, when winter damage is cut out.

Common lavender is frequently seen in gardens as an untidy sprawling bush, due entirely to lack of pruning. During spring, just prior to growth commencing, bushes should be clipped hard, in the course of which old flower spikes are removed and most of the previous year's growth. Neglected bushes need very hard pruning but it is better done in two or three stages and not all at once.

Lavatera (tree mallow) DS Slightly tender shrubs needing full sun and a rather poor, well-drained soil. Trim to shape.

73

Ledum ES   Pruning should be unnecessary except to thin and to remove dead wood. If this becomes excessive it is an indication that all is not well.

Leiophyllum ES   Classed with the heathers, which it closely resembles, it is treated in the same way. Trim over with a pair of shears in spring.

Leucothoë ES   Occasionally it may be necessary to remove at ground-level old wood and any unsightly stems in spring.

Ligustrum (privet) E/DS   Privets are best known as hedging plants though specimens are sometimes used in topiary. Grown for foliage, flowers or fruit they can make handsome shrubs or even small trees. Shrubs are left to develop several leaders and established pruning consists of trimming to shape and thinning in March. Strong-growing forms can be trained to a single leader with all side shoots retained but shortened, and eventually removed.

Lonicera (honeysuckle) D/ES/Cl   Shrubby honeysuckles should, after blossoming, be trimmed to shape and the branches which have flowered should be removed. If a feature is to be made of the berries, pruning should be delayed until the winter, or spring for evergreens.

It is not necessary to prune climbers every year unless space is restricted. Climbers can be separated into two groups; those flowering on current season's growth are pruned in the winter, when necessary, cutting back hard to a framework; those flowering on one-year-old wood are pruned after flowering when those shoots which have flowered are removed, together with crowded growth.

Magnolia E/DS/T   Branches tend to be pithy and bark is easily damaged if blunt or badly set tools are used. Pruning is best carried out in summer when new growth is complete; dormant wood is slow to heal and die-back, following winter pruning, is common.

Tree magnolias should be kept to a single leader on which the side shoots are shortened and eventually removed. Young

74

growth is frequently damaged by late frosts and if the leader is destroyed a new one will have to be trained in.

Magnolia grandiflora is still considered as a wall shrub but is really unsuitable in such a position for its large leaves cause undue shading, and with age the trunks become increasingly difficult to keep tied back. Wall-trained *M. grandiflora* does perhaps flower more abundantly than a free-standing tree so if training is undertaken for this reason a well-spaced framework must be provided. This can be fan-shaped or in tiers, ensuring that the base of the wall is kept clothed. Established pruning means removing old flower heads and thinning and cutting away shoots coming from the wall in spring.

Bush magnolia need little attention, although dead-heading is desirable for many kinds produce copious quantities of fruit which, if left to develop, reduces vigour. When dead-heading, cut rather than break off the spent flowers for the new growth buds are just behind the flowers. *M. × soulangiana* varieties have a tendency to produce masses of young growth along the main stem; this should be rubbed off as it appears.

Mahonia ES   Several of the low-growing kinds can be used for ground cover, which can be kept low and thick if sheared off just above ground-level every three or four years; if not growing strongly remove some of the oldest stems and trim back remaining growth. Other forms need only occasional pruning when the oldest stems are cut out at ground-level in the spring.

Malus (crab apple) DT   Some species are raised from seed and therefore on their own roots, but many species and all cultivars are grafted on to one of the fruit rootstocks which controls the ultimate size of the tree. Most crab apples are trained as standards although they can also be trained to a central leader. Once the framework has formed, there is little pruning required beyond the removal of crossing branches.

Mespilus (medlar) DT   The enjoyment of the fruit of medlar is an acquired taste at present out of favour and this plant is now grown mainly as an ornamental. Once a framework has been formed, either as a standard or with a central leader, all that is necessary is to remove crossing branches.

Olearia ES/T   Most species are tender and are often planted as free-standing shrubs at the foot of a wall. *O. haastii* and *O. macrodonta* are two of the hardiest species, needing no protection. Those which flower early in the year are pruned after flowering when old flower shoots are removed and the bush is trimmed to shape. Those flowering late are pruned in May, again old flower stalks are removed and bushes are trimmed to shape.

Osmanthus ES/T   Most species are tender and need wall protection. *O. delavayi* and *O. heterophyllus* are the hardiest, the former flowering in spring, the latter in late autumn. The early flowers are trimmed after flowering, the late flowers in May just before growth begins.

Osmarea ES×   A hardy floriferous shrub that should be trimmed to shape after flowering.

Osmaronia DS   Has a suckering habit and eventually forms large clumps. This shrub, which flowers early in the year, should have the oldest stems, and any weak ones, removed after flowering.

Pachysandra ES   Widely grown for ground cover. Pruning is only necessary if stems become bare and woody or foliage thin. Shear over a few inches above ground-level in spring.

Paeonia (tree peony) DS   Most species are herbaceous, only a few having woody stems. Occasionally take out some of the old stems at ground-level if they become gaunt; remove dead flowers and fruiting heads after flowering; if seeds are wanted, delay until these have been shed. Towards the end of a wet summer some thinning of lush growth will aid the ripening of wood.

Parrotia DS/T   A shrub grown for its early flowers and colourful bark, but particularly for its gorgeous autumn colour. A strong-growing shrub with tiered branches which can become tree-like. It can be trained to a central leader with all side shoots retained, or it can be allowed to develop naturally.

76

Parrotia persica produces masses of branches which should be thinned in winter or following flowering. Cut back to a point where there is another branch.

Parthenocissus DCl   This genus includes the Virginia creeper. All are vigorous climbers which attach themselves to supports by means of tendrils on which there are suckers. Unless given plenty of space (as on an old tree) they can be invasive, shutting out light from windows and dislodging slates, gutters and down-pipes. Where possible an annual reduction of growth is desirable, at the least cutting well back from windows, doors, pipes, gutters and roof. Cut out old wood in winter, remembering that it is only young shoots which are able to attach themselves to supports.

Passiflora (passion flower) D/ECl   All species are tender and even *P. caerulea*, the hardiest, can be damaged by winter cold. Train a well-spaced framework to cover a wall, then thin out crowded growth and drastically reduce during May.

Paulownia DS   Each year in spring, cut all stems to ground level and reduce the resulting shoots to three or five. Take care not to damage the roots otherwise these will sucker most profusely.

Pernettya ES   A suckering shrub grown for its attractive show of fruits which remain largely untouched by birds. In good conditions it can become rather invasive and some restriction may be desirable; otherwise occasionally remove some of the oldest wood in spring.

Philadelphus (mock orange) DS   If there is plenty of space, these shrubs can be grown with the minimum of pruning, removing blind shoots from the centre of the bush and reducing surplus shoots. When space is limited, remove branches that have carried flowers and thin out surplus shoots in summer.

Phillyrea ES   Trim to shape and thin out if crowded, in spring.

77

Phlomis ES   Only some species are woody and most of these are slightly tender, needing full sun and a warm position. Cut out or cut back old flowering stems and thin growth in spring.

Photinia ES   All species are somewhat tender and are often grown on a south wall. Valued more for their young red foliage than for their flowers which are not very interesting. In April all growth is trimmed back to about half of that produced in the previous year.

Phygelius DS   The tops are often killed in the winter and, in the manner of herbaceous plants, growth is produced from beneath ground-level. If the tops do survive they should be cut away, for flowering is on current season's growth.

Pieris ES   Little pruning is necessary except to dead-head, thin and trim. Young non-flowering growth of *P. forrestii* is a brilliant red which fades to green as it ages. A second flush of brilliant growth can be obtained by the (unorthodox) practice of trimming back the shoots when the leaves have turned green.

Pittosporum ES   Most species are tender, *P. tenuifolium* being the hardiest of them. Plant in a protected place out of cold winds. Trim to shape in April, cutting out winter damage and thinning.

Polygonum DCl   *P. baldschuanicum*, the Russian vine, is commonly grown for screening. Its rampant habit makes it ideal for this purpose but unless there is plenty of space its nature can be an embarrassment. Each year, in March, remove shoots that are likely to encroach, drastically reduce and thin out, cutting as near to the ground as possible.

Potentilla DS   Untidy growers that tend to collect dead leaves and accumulate a mass of dead or blind twigs. Clear out centres of bushes in March and reduce the previous year's growth by a half.

Prunus D/ES/T   There are many kinds of *Prunus* of differing

78

size, shape and habit, and all of them susceptible to silver leaf disease. Pruning of most species is kept to a minimum after building up a framework. Those which make trees are trained to a central leader.

Japanese cherries are grafted, sometimes low down but most often on to stems of varying lengths. Heads are often one-sided and by judicious pruning this should be corrected so as to produce a well-spaced and balanced spread.

Ornamental peaches, almonds and their hybrids should have a portion of wood which has flowered removed in spring. Sometimes they are fan-trained against a wall; after building up a framework, remove shoots which have flowered. *Prunus triloba, glandulosa* and their forms are also grown against walls, and following the completion of a well-spaced framework, all side shoots are cut hard back to this after flowering.

Some kinds, eg *P. serrula*, are grown for their barks. Train a central leader and expose the trunk as soon as possible. There are a number of weeping forms of cherries of various species and cv groups. These may be low grafted but are most often grafted high. Support the main stem with a stake and ensure that there is a sufficient length of trunk to allow the pendant branches to hang gracefully. If the main stem is not long enough train in a leader, reducing the framework until sufficient length has been gained, then train in a new framework. The evergreen species are most often grown as hedges though they can be grown as specimen plants. Keep to a single leader, retaining side shoots, and trim to shape in spring.

Pyracantha (firethorn) ES Grown against a north or east wall, for which its habit is well suited. During training select several leaders, spacing them wide enough apart to allow side branches to cover their allotted space without overcrowding. The main leaders should be secured in position, for though they keep close to the wall they tend to fall away with age. During April, cut back any shoots coming away from the wall, thin out crowded shoots and trim back. As the leaders become old, select and train in new ones; when these are established the old can be removed.

Pyracanthas are perfectly well suited for growing as free-standing shrubs; three or five leaders should be selected and well spaced. In April open up the centre of the bush, thin out crowded shoots and trim to shape.

Pyrus (pear) DT   Train to a single leader. No regular pruning is necessary beyond the removal of crossing branches. *P. salicifolia*, and especially its weeping form, need to have the leader secured to a stake and should be trained to an 8ft stem before a framework is allowed to develop.

All species of *Pyrus* are susceptible to fireblight.

Rhamnus DS   In general these shrubs should be allowed to develop naturally, though a few of the stronger species can be trained to a central leader and feathered. During February thin crowded shoots; forms with fancy leaves can be trimmed back moderately hard.

Rhododendron E/DS   Azaleas, which form a series among the *Rhododendron* species, are included here. There are very many species and hybrids of varying sizes, shapes, habits, shape of flowers and degrees of hardiness. It is important when transplanting to replant to the same depth as previously. Too deep planting has an adverse effect, causing a sickly appearance and the dying out of parts of the shrub.

Many hybrids and some species are grafted and any suckers which arise from the rootstock should be removed as they appear; if left they grow away at the expense of the plant. Carry out dead-heading annually and at the same time trim back any shoot growing out of alignment. With age, some rhododendrons become too tall, bare at the base, or their shape falls away; these can be cut back really hard after flowering.

Bud blast is a disease which kills the flower buds; remove and burn infected buds.

Rhus DS/T   Gardeners are warned that some species can cause a skin rash. People vary in their sensitivity to different species but *R. vernix*, *toxicodendron* and *succedanea* are most likely to cause irritation. When pruning any species of *Rhus*, wear thick gloves, cover all bare parts of the body and wear overalls.

Tree forms are kept to a single leader and feathered. Shrubs can be left unpruned, thinning out crowded shoots in March. *R. typhina* and *glabra* and their forms are usually grown mainly for their foliage, either summer or autumn; the amount and size can be increased by pruning in the winter.

Ribes (currants) D/ES   A few species are tender. Mostly they flower on one-year-old wood, and after flowering the shoots which have borne flowers are removed. Some form spurs and a framework should be formed on a short leg, and well spaced. During the winter open up the centre of the bush and cut back young growth to within two or three buds of the main stems. Evergreen kinds are little pruned except to thin, if required, in spring.

Romneya (tree poppy) ES   Rather succulent, behaving often as an herbaceous plant with growth that dies back to a root-stock in winter. It is usually planted against the side of a path because its roots like a cool soil, but has the disconcerting habit of disappearing from the place chosen for it and reappearing elsewhere. In March or April, just prior to the commencement of growth, reduce any surviving shoots and cut out any old ones.

Rosmarinus (rosemary) ES   Whilst reasonably hardy, rosemary may suffer in an extra cold winter; prostrate forms, if left unsheltered, can be killed or seriously damaged in even averagely cold weather. Bushes can be trimmed to shape in April but it is preferable to wait until after the first flush of flowers is over.

Rubus (brambles) D/ES   A few of the evergreen species are tender and need wall protection. Most species have a stool-like or even suckering habit, but some of the deciduous kinds have canes of only two years' duration.

Brambles with coloured stems are cut to ground-level in March, and young growth drastically thinned out in established clumps. Species grown for their flowers or fruit are pruned during the winter. If stems are of two-year duration only, those shoots which have flowered are removed; if stems are longer lived, those which have flowered should be cut back.

Ruscus (butcher's broom) LS   Remove discoloured shoots and occasionally some of the old wood in spring.

Ruta (rue) ES   All species are slightly tender and likely to be damaged in a cold winter. All are short lived and replacements should be kept available for replanting. Common rue (*R. graveolens*) is an untidy grower and needs drastic thinning in May.

Salix (willow) DS/T   Willows vary from tiny shrubs to large trees, all liking a moist soil. Strong-growing kinds are trained to a single leader; smaller kinds can be similarly treated but with all side shoots retained although reduced. There is a tendency for branches to be damaged or lost in gales so space out the main branches; prevent undue extension and avoid narrow crotches.

Shrubs can be treated as already described or can be allowed several leaders. When willows are grown especially for catkins or foliage, best produced on young wood, cut hard back to within a few inches of the base of the previous year's growth, just before growth commences. When grown for their coloured stems, cut to ground-level or to within a few buds of a framework in March. Small growing and prostrate kinds are rarely pruned except to remove dead wood or to thin.

Santolina (lavender cotton) ES   Fragrant shrub with grey-white leaves, grown for its foliage rather than its yellow flowers which, however, have some attraction. Unpruned bushes sprawl untidily and are short lived. After flowering, the old flower stems should be removed and the bushes trimmed back. When growing just for foliage, trimming is carried out in April and most of the previous year's growth is removed; a second trimming is desirable as the flower buds appear.

Sarcococca ES   Restrict if clumps become invasive; otherwise just cut out old gaunt stems, or if clumps become untidy

82

shear back to within a few inches of ground-level in spring.

Schizophragma DCl   A climber which supports itself by producing roots on its young shoots. Space out these shoots as they begin to grow, pointing them in the desired direction; if they grow wrongly they have to be pulled off the wall and cannot be made to refix themselves. Once the support has been covered, branching occurs and flowering begins. Old flower shoots should be removed in March, being cut back as near as possible to the main framework.

Senecio ES   Many species are tender and need protection of a wall; in late spring remove winter damage and thin out crowded shoots. Free-standing shrubs are similarly treated earlier, when they are trimmed to shape, thinned, and old flower stalks removed.

Skimmia ES   Occasionally remove some of the oldest wood and if necessary trim to shape in spring.

Spartium (Spanish broom) LS   Its pithy stems tend to be soft and easily damaged if growing in shade or a rich soil. Trim shoots hard back to a framework in spring.

Spiraea DS   Some species flower on one-year wood, eg *S.* × *vanhouttei* and × *arguta*; these are cut back to where new growth is developing following flowering. Others such as *S.* × *bumalda*, *S. japonica* and *S. douglasii* flower on current season's growth and are pruned to within a few inches of ground-level during February.

Stachyurus DS   Occasionally remove some of the old wood, preferably in autumn.

Staphylea DS   Generally these have a suckering habit. During the winter remove some of the oldest wood, reducing the remainder and trimming to shape.

Stephanandra DS   Grown more for the graceful habit of stems and foliage rather than for flowers. During March

83

remove some of the oldest stems carefully, trimming and thinning the remainder so as to retain the grace of habit.

Stranvaesia ES   Following training, thin out shoots in spring if crowded.

Styrax DS/T   The strongest members should be trained to a single leader with all side shoots retained, but thinned if too crowded. The less vigorous kinds can be treated in the same way, or several leaders can be permitted. Prune in spring, cutting out crowded branches and keeping the centres of bushes open. Trimming may be necessary again if late frost causes damage.

Symphoricarpos DS   All species have a suckering habit which can be invasive in a good soil; if so, clumps must be restricted. During March, remove the oldest and weakest shoots, thinning the remainder.

Syringa (lilac) DS/T   If space is not limited, little pruning is required except for dead-heading and the removal of blind shoots from the centre of bushes. In small gardens there should be a reduction of some of the shoots and some trimming following dead-heading.

The stronger kinds will make small trees if trained and kept to a single leader; this needs regular attention because of the forking habit of lilac. Most cultivars of lilac are grafted either on to privet or wild lilac; suckers from the former stock are easy to recognise but those of the latter are not, therefore any shoot which emerges from beneath ground-level should be removed at the point of origin.

Tamarix DS/T   Some flower on one-year-old wood and these should be pruned following flowering, the wood which has flowered being removed and the resulting growths thinned. Others flower in late summer or autumn and these are pruned hard in March, being cut back to a framework; some thinning of resulting growth is desirable. The strongest kinds can be trained into small trees by selecting a central leader and reducing side shoots.

84

Teucrium (germander) ES   Some species are tender and need protection. All tend to sprawl and are untidy growers. In spring cut back to shape and keep within bounds.

Thymus ES   The mat types may need occasional attention to remove dead wood, but if this becomes excessive the entire planting should be lifted and renewed. Those forming shrubs, eg the common thyme *T. vulgaris*, are pruned in April when there is a thinning of shoots and most of the previous year's growth is trimmed back.

Vaccinium E/DS   Occasionally some thinning may be required and trimming to shape. This is best done in early spring.

Viburnum D/ES   A few species are tender and need wall protection. Some of the winter flowerers also need protection for their flowers. Little pruning is necessary but occasionally some of the oldest wood is removed and it may be desirable to trim to shape following a heavy fruit set. Winter flowerers are pruned in April or May; summer flowerers are cut in February or March, and evergreens are trimmed in April.

Vitex DS/T   All species flower late and are slightly tender; they are therefore planted against a wall for protection. Flowering is on current season's growth and in April all shoots are pruned hard back to a framework.

Vitis DCl   If growing over a tree, no pruning is required. If on a wall, fence or pergola where space is limited, after training in several rods all side shoots are cut back to one or two buds of these in the winter. Do not delay pruning otherwise bleeding will occur.

Wisteria DCl/S   A very popular and beautiful shrub that is too often planted where there is insufficient space or where no attention is given to pruning. All species are vigorous and if left to their own devices their long trails can dislodge slates, gutter and down-pipes. Following planting, cut back stems by half, and continue to do this each spring until a well-spaced framework has been trained in. In July all young shoots are

85

cut back to four or five buds, and in winter these shoots are reduced to two or three buds. This builds up a spur system and reduces extension growth, so encouraging the greatest number of flowers.

A free-standing shrub can be produced from a wisteria. Train in five leaders, cutting back to 3ft in the first winter; the next winter cut the new extension growth back to no more than 3ft. Some support will be necessary and can be provided by attaching the framework, maypole-fashion, to a central leader. Prune all side shoots, as already described, in July and February.

If trained over a tree no pruning is necessary.

Zenobia DS   These shrubs have a suckering habit. Occasionally remove some of the oldest wood, tipping shoots in March. Dead-head and at the same time cut back to where new growth is breaking.

7

Apples and Pears

The principles and practice of pruning are put to the test with tree fruits more than with flowering shrubs or hedges. The latter need to be restrained and shaped but a few ill-considered cuts—or even pruning skipped for a year—will not result in lasting harm. The fruit tree is less amenable to the casual approach. To persuade it to produce regular crops from an early age it must be 'built' into a fruit production unit—often of unnatural shape—and every ˛piece of growth must be assessed for its ability to increase fruiting potential.

This begins with the tree in the fruit nursery. These days trees of the majority of crop fruits are rarely supplied on their own roots. The nurseryman has a choice of rootstocks which limit the vigour of the variety and encourage it to crop at an early date. Thus an apple variety (the scion) is budded or grafted on to a semi-dwarfing or dwarfing root (the stock) of the same family to produce a tree that remains 'bush' size. The gardener is advised to specify a bush tree when ordering apples or pears. Clearly there is no point in having a tall, vigorous tree that requires a ladder for pruning and picking.

The year after budding or grafting, the scion bud sends up a 'wand' of growth, and this first-year tree is known as a 'maiden'. These can be purchased by the gardener who wishes to carry out the critical first phase of training which is to secure the basic framework of branches. Alternatively this is done by the nurseryman, and the gardener buys a two- or three-year-old tree at a correspondingly increased price.

Before detailing the pruning procedure it is important to appreciate why a tree must be carefully 'built' from infancy. A good fruit-producing unit is a bush form with branches radiating around the trunk at a roughly equal distance apart. These branches should emerge from the trunk as close to the horizontal as possible—that is, approaching an angle of 90° with the trunk. Throughout its development, light and air must have direct access to all parts of the tree, particularly the centre, so that complete pollination and ripening take place. A dense tree or one that is allowed to shoot up in columnar fashion is not efficient in the above respects; narrow-angle branches are more likely to split away under the weight of a heavy crop, and conditions in the dense centre favour the

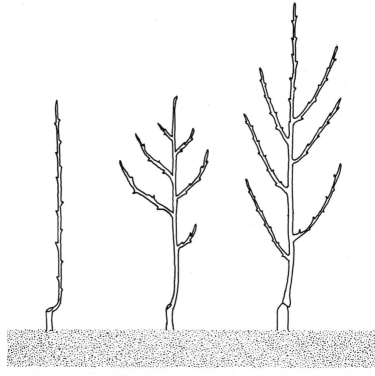

Types of fruit trees as usually purchased. *Left* a maiden, *centre* a feathered maiden, and *right* a two-year whip growth.

development of pests and diseases.

The continuing aim of fruit-tree pruning—especially of apples and pears—is to keep the tree balanced in shape, and balanced in the proportions of old and young wood. 'Cutting back' is too simple a definition of pruning to apply to tree fruits. Such an arbitrary approach will only serve to delay and reduce the yield of fruit. An unpruned tree, if it is on dwarfing stock, will fruit early in its life and keep bearing. But—and this is why we prune—it will soon become crowded with growths, unhealthy, and bear small (if numerous) fruits irregularly.

So the gardener seeks a compromise by building a tree of manageable shape in the early years, and thereafter by selective pruning maintaining the same proportions while it grows bigger.

An important qualification is that different varieties have different natural growth habits which lend themselves to one form of training and pruning rather than another once the framework is established.

Winter pruning of apples and pears can be tackled after leaf fall and is better done early in the winter than late. Similarly a young tree is best planted and cut back in early winter. Summer pruning, which helps to control vigour and exposes ripening fruit to sunlight, is carried out in the height of the season.

We have seen that a tree may be purchased as a 'maiden' or as a two- or three-year-old. The maiden comes as a single 'wand' of growth which must be cut back after planting. A bush tree is the only sensible shape for the modern garden and this means cutting back to leave a stem of about 2ft 6in, using a sharp pocket knife, or equally sharp secateurs. From below this cut in the following spring the growth buds will extend as shoots, the strongest just below the cut, the others in descending order of vigour. The top three shoots are retained as prospective branches of the tree. Ideally these branches should emerge at a wide angle from the stem, but it so happens that the topmost bud always emerges at a narrow angle and grows up almost vertically. However, the next bud down makes a better angle, so a way has been devised of rejecting the unsuitable top bud. Before the buds break, a small piece of

89

wood is nicked out just below the top bud, so diverting most of the sap energy to buds below. The following winter the stub above the new top shoot is cleanly cut away. If any of the three top buds is close to its neighbour it is best cut out and another lower one allowed to grow.

We have reached the stage at which three shoots—framework branches—have been secured, either in the nursery before purchase or by the gardener. In the winter following their extension each of the three is cut back by about two-thirds. If possible choose a point above an outward-facing bud and always cut at a slight slope away from the bud.

From below this cut at least two shoots can be expected to extend from each parent branch. So the following winter there are six more branches (six is a good number), which this time are cut back by half their length. One more year's development gives an 'adult' tree with an optimum of twelve branches spaced evenly all round with none growing into the centre.

The aim of subsequent pruning

After this, hard pruning ceases and attention is directed towards keeping a balance between old and young wood. It is important to recognise by looking at the winter buds whether they will make growth shoots or flowers and fruit. Growth buds are slim and pressed tightly to the stem, while fruit buds are fatter and stand more away from the stem.

Look at a branch in winter that has been growing (and been pruned) for three years. The top section will be bearing mainly growth buds, the middle section mainly fruit buds, and the oldest section will have groups of fruit buds called spurs. With the renewal pruning method to be described shortly, this type of branch is kept for several years until replaced by a younger cropping unit. As well as vigorous and potentially useful laterals from the main branches, short and weak growths will also appear. Invariably these should be pruned hard back—by at least two-thirds—for they have no future as replacement branches. It is a safe rule of thumb to prune weak growth hard and strong growth lightly once the tree framework has been formed. Any attempt to control vigorous growth by hard

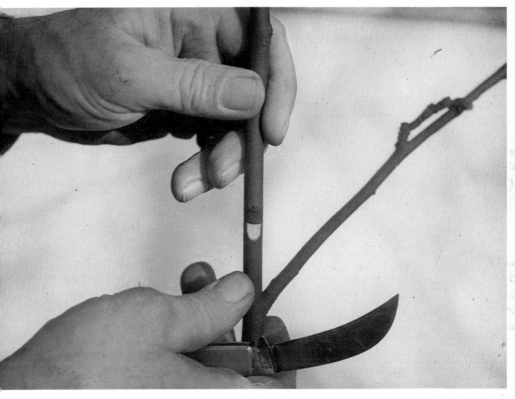

Notching a young apple. The point of this operation is to encourage the branches to grow more horizontally than they would otherwise. It is usually used in training cordons.

pruning will be met by an even more vigorous response by the tree. On the other hand there is a chance that stronger growth will result from the hard cutting-back of a weak shoot.

The following section deals specifically with apple-tree pruning. Just as a number of trained tree shapes have become accepted as distinct forms (bush, dwarf pyramid, cordon etc), so a number of pruning methods have been developed to deal with certain training systems or with certain varieties. Essentially these can be narrowed down to two: established spur pruning and renewal pruning. The latter is the more natural approach with a bush tree. However, variety has an influence on choice, and the firm UK favourite Cox's Orange Pippin has growth that lends itself to spur pruning as does the US variety Yellow Delicious. At the other extreme, many varieties tend to bear fruit towards the tips of branches. Clearly all laterals should not be cut hard back to form spurs, and even renewal pruning entails shortening most shoots. Both methods would reduce the crop to a greater or lesser extent. Thus with these tip-bearers and other very vigorous varieties it is best to restrict pruning to the removal of dead, competing and inward-pointing wood each winter.

Renewal pruning of apple trees

Renewal pruning suits most bush apple trees. While the variety Cox lends itself to a spur-pruning system, it can also be successfully pruned by the renewal method. In its simplest form the method involves the winter pruning of some new growth and shoots that have carried fruit. Leading lateral branches are left unpruned in order to develop fruit buds along their length. When they are brought down near the ground by the weight of fruit it is time to replace them. For this purpose a sub-lateral, upward growing and suitably positioned, has been kept lightly pruned. The old branch is cut cleanly away at its junction with the replacement leader.

Shoots are not pruned until after they have borne fruit, but once this has occurred (on two-year-old wood) the shoot is ready to be renewed. This is done by cutting it back to within two buds of the main branch. Renewal of fruiting wood is the

92

aim of the system. Young shoots arising directly (that is, not associated with wood that has borne fruit) are nearly all left unpruned in order to make fruiting wood the following year. But a minority are cut hard back to two buds. Temper this cutting back according to tree vigour. If the tree is vigorous leave a number of these shoots unpruned each year. Hard pruning of nearly all new shoots is the rule on weaker-growing trees.

This 'staggering' of shoot pruning helps to overcome the tendency known as biennial bearing—heavy crop one year, none the next.

Established spur pruning

In contrast to the renewal method, fruit-bearing wood is left to develop a fruiting spur system with established spur pruning, instead of being replaced after fruiting. Each new shoot is cut back according to its vigour: to four or five buds if vigorous, to one or two if weak.

In future years growth shoots from this spur are treated similarly, with the result that a group of spurs consisting almost entirely of fruit buds is built up. Clearly some shoots must be treated differently, and the leading shoots on branches are only lightly pruned by the removal of the top inch or two. And a minority of shoots of medium vigour are not spurred back until they have fruited (which will happen earlier than on spurred shoots).

Vary the number of spurred and unpruned shoots according to tree vigour, spurring weak growth and sparing the strongest. Spur systems get crowded after a few years and themselves need pruning. Thin out up to half of the clusters to allow space for fruit development and light for ripening.

Summer pruning

Summer pruning is carried out about a month before a variety is picked – usually from July to August – and at such a time there should be little if any regrowth from the cut shoots. Its result is to expose fruit and wood to the beneficial effect of light and air; it can reduce pest or disease incidence and will give a 'check' to vigour. Weakly growing trees should not be summer pruned. So shorten new shoots to 3in wherever this will expose ripening fruit.

Rejuvenating an old tree
Old apple and pear trees are often found in a neglected state, and fit at first sight only for grubbing out. However, with

a

Removing a large limb from a mature tree. Firstly a cut is made at some distance from the main stem, and the weight of the branch removed. If any tearing occurs it will not affect the final pruned surface. The stump of the branch is then removed flush with the main stem, and the cut surface pared with a pruning knife until it is smooth. Finally the wound is painted with a pruning compound, which prevents diseases entering the exposed wood and acts as a temporary bark until the tree's own bark grows across the wound.

remedial pruning over a period of years such trees can be given a new lease of life. Neglect and abuse may have resulted in one of two ways. Where no pruning has taken place for years the tree will be overgrown with worn-out fruiting spur systems. The other possibility is that the tree has been 'hacked' instead of pruned so that it is a mass of congested shoots and quite fruitless.

In the first case, a procedure known as de-horning is

adopted. This is drastic pruning and involves cutting out one or two branches each year as close to the crotch of the tree as need be. Initially remove branches that crowd the centre, and later thin out the periphery if necessary. Aim to reduce overall height by cutting to a point where a lower branch can take over. Cut cleanly at these junctions, making sure that the wound is properly sealed. If there are not many branches to

c

d

e

f

be removed but spur clusters are crowded on old wood, thin out these clusters by half over a period of some four winters.

A tree that has been hacked to resemble a pollarded willow again needs whole branches cut out before shoot thinning is tackled on the remainder. Encourage a new framework of well-placed branches by selecting some of the best-placed shoots to be new leaders and tipping them. Leave enough of the others as laterals which will make fruit buds if left un-pruned. Cut out at their base surplus 'watershoots' from old wood.

Pears

Fruit spurs form more easily and abundantly on pears than on apples, so that they are well suited to be trained in shapes such as cordon or espalier and pruned by the established spur system (described on page 93). Bush trees can also be formed without any trouble, along the lines described for apples. With pears it is generally easier to achieve the ideal 'goblet' shape with an open centre.

To form a low-growing bush from a maiden tree, allow three well-spaced shoots to develop after cutting back, then double the number by pruning each to two buds. Treat further growth on established-spur-principles described below.

Summer pruning is of more benefit to pears than apples, and is most important on trees trained to special shapes. The method is to reduce weaker side shoots to four leaves and stronger ones to six leaves. This is followed up by winter spur pruning back to two buds. As with apples, a minority of shoots can be left unpruned for a year to ensure a succession of fruit buds.

Leaders need to be cut back by a third in winter (with most apple varieties they are just tipped). Thick spur clusters soon develop on pears and need to be thinned progressively.

Special tree shapes

Dwarf pyramid By definition these trees are dwarf and pyramidal in shape. Dwarfness comes from the rootstock, and the best ones for this form of tree will be recommended by the nursery. In contrast to an open-centred bush tree, the central leader must be retained to serve as the 'spinal column' of the pyramid. If a maiden is planted and then cut back in the normal way, the top buds must be stimulated into strong growth. The top one will be vigorous enough, but the next three or four can be encouraged by nicking out a small piece of bark above each one.

In the early winter of the following year these shoots are pruned back by half, cutting to a bud on the underside so that the shoots tend to grow out at a wide angle. Continue to winter prune the central leader so that it maintains vigorous vertical growth and keep the extension growth of the other main branches in proportion so that the shape continues to resemble a Christmas tree. As the leaders extend, tiers of side shoots will develop. Once the lowest side shoots have borne fruit all side shoots are summer pruned and spurred back in winter as described earlier for apples and pears. A pattern develops of tiers of laterals with sub-laterals.

Once the central leader has reached the maximum height desired, the relatively hard winter pruning of leaders ceases.

Cordon   As with other restricted tree forms, trees to be grown as cordons should be on a dwarfing rootstock and of an amenable variety. Ask your nurseryman for suitable varieties. The various cordon shapes and espalier trees require a supporting framework of posts and wire, which is best set up before the row is planted. Wires can also be fixed directly to a garden wall. There is little point in choosing a space-saving tree form unless several are planted, and this makes economical use of the posts and wire. These must be stout and durable, and wood posts—though the best looking—will need replacing one day. Angle-iron or old piping is probably best and needs to be sunk deeply or buried in concrete. Concrete posts will also serve, though they tend to be bulky. Use strong wire and intermediate supports every 3ft or so. Wires at 2, 3, 4 and 5ft from the ground provide a good supporting system.

Best known of the variations on the cordon theme is the oblique cordon, and this is considered the best for the average garden. More space is required by the single U-cordon, which itself can be compounded into a double U-cordon.

The oblique cordon begins life as a single stem and remains

97

De-horning a pear tree.

Summer pruning a pear tree. This operation is fully described in the text.

thus throughout its cropping life. To form such a cordon of your own, start with a maiden tree and plant it close to the wire at an angle of 45° to the ground. Allow 3ft between each tree and plant so that the graft union (visible as a swelling just above the soil mark on the stem) faces the ground. This is done because the base of the tree will be under pressure and the union ·might split if facing upwards. With each cordon a bamboo cane is required, tied to the wire at a 45° angle, to which the maiden tree is secured with soft string.

The leading growth is allowed to extend each year, and cane and cordon are lowered by about 5° when the top wire is reached. This procedure reduces vigour and leads to plentiful fruit-bud formation. Summer pruning is the main treatment for a cordon. It begins the summer after planting when shoots are shortened back to four or five leaves in mid-summer. In winter they are spurred back further. Thus spur systems develop on the lowest part of the stem and extend upwards each year. By the time most of the cordon is clothed with fruit spurs it is time to practise spur thinning on the oldest.

As always, use discretion in pruning according to tree vigour, cutting back thin weak shoots harder than average and very strong ones less hard. This is a simple and rewarding way to grow apples or pears in a small garden.

To make a single U-cordon, the maiden tree is cut back to about 1ft and two resulting shoots are allowed to extend in opposite directions, then tied to canes on a wire 1ft above ground. After about 6in of growth has been tied to the canes the shoots are turned upwards and tied to upright canes. In winter they are pruned by about one-third. In successive winters they are just tipped, while all side shoots are summer and winter pruned to make spurs. Skill is exercised in keeping both arms of the U at the same height, and there is twice the work in the double U-cordon.

Espalier This horizontally spreading shape requires around 15ft of wall or post-and-wire space per tree. The system is built up in tiers, tapering to the top. A maiden is cut back to about 18in, to a bud above a pair lying opposite each other. The terminal bud and the two below are allowed to grow, the terminal being tied to a vertical cane on the wire-supporting framework, the two opposite shoots to canes at an angle of about 45° from the leader in order not to weaken them by making them horizontal at once. They are lowered to the bottom wire at the end of the first growing season, but if one is weaker it is only partially lowered. The vertical leader is winter pruned back to about 2ft.

During the next growing season, two more suitably placed opposite shoots on the vertical leader are chosen as the second tier of the espalier, and other shoots in the same region are pinched hard back while young. In this and future years all side shoots from the tiered branches are summer pruned according to vigour, and spurred back in winter.

The formation of each tier follows the same pattern as the first: namely, supporting the opposing shoots first at 45° then lowering them to the horizontal while keeping a balance for vigour.

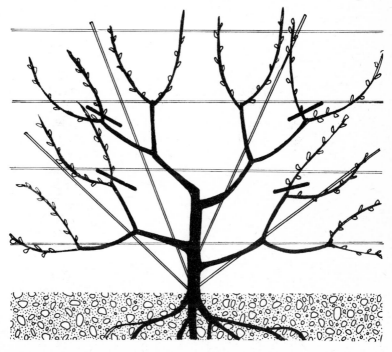

Canes used in the training of a fan-trained fruit tree.

101

a

b

c

Cordon apples. The first two pictures show the training pruning of young maiden cordons, the third picture a row of well-trained established cordons.

8
Plums and Cherries

Pruning risks for plums

Plum pruning is not without risk—to the tree. The spores of silver leaf fungus disease may gain entry through pruning cuts, and this disease is capable of killing a tree. As the name implies, leaves on affected branches take on a silvery appearance by comparison with healthy leaves.

Suspect the disease if you see much dead wood in a plum tree. If towards the end of the year small bracket fungi are produced on the dead wood it is almost certain that silver leaf is the cause. For confirmation, cut into suspected wood and look for a dark ring staining the wood; this is a sure sign that the fungus is present.

First action with an established plum or gage tree in the garden is to cut all dead branches back to healthy wood, preferably by mid-summer, certainly before the end of summer. If they prove to be silver leaf infected, cut back until no stain can be seen in the wood. Then paint the cut surfaces with a pruning compound, and burn the prunings immediately.

Because of the risk of introducing this disease, all bush, half-standard or standard plum trees should be pruned as little as possible. What pruning is necessary should be carried out in early summer when the cuts heal rapidly and silver leaf infection is least likely. All that is required is to remove crossing branches that may rub together and a few others that may be crowding the centre of the tree. Some varieties have a pendulous habit and the tips of a few branches may have to be cut back. Plums fruit on wood produced in the previous year and on spurs on older branches. If pruning in early summer means the removal of branches bearing unripe plums, the operation can be delayed until immediately after picking.

Plums are particularly prone to branch splitting, especially if the crop is heavy, and it is wise to have some props handy to support laden branches in a good year. However, if the worst happens, remove the broken branch at once and cover all damaged surfaces with wound paint.

Establishment of a bush plum

In the average garden a bush plum, with 2–3ft of trunk before the branches begin, is the best shape. Half-standards, with a 4ft trunk, are useful for the more spreading varieties such as the popular Victoria. Plums are not suitable for growing in restricted forms such as cordon or espalier.

Nurserymen will supply one-year-old trees (maidens) or older trees on which a framework of branches has already been formed. If a two- to three-year-old tree is purchased, no pruning will be required until the spring a year after planting. To produce a bush tree from a maiden, the stem must be cut back to just above a bud, about 9in above the desired position of the lowest branch. This is done after planting, in the spring and before bud burst. Small shoots low on the stem can be left, as they help to build up the tree until a number of strong branches have been formed. In summer shorten them back to four or five leaves, and after two to three years remove them completely.

Pruning in the second year involves the selection of the main branches. A number of strong shoots should have formed near the head of the tree, and about four of similar strength and evenly spaced round the stem are selected. These young branches ideally should make an angle as near as possible to 90° with the main stem. Such branches will be able to support a heavy weight of fruit, while those emerging at a narrow angle will be weak and prone to split. The chosen wide-angled branches are cut back in spring to a bud about halfway along their length while the remainder which form narrow angles and are badly placed are removed entirely.

In the third year, leaders (strong-growing branches) are cut back by half the growth they made in the previous year, and crossing and crowded shoots are removed. In subsequent years pruning is carried out in June or July and only involves the removal of dead, broken, crossing and crowded shoots as already mentioned.

Cherries

There are two distinct types of cherry: the sweet or dessert kind, and the acid cherry, of which the popular Montmorency is well known. With neither of them is winter pruning carried out owing to the risk of silver leaf disease infection.

Sweet cherries　These are not suitable for the smaller garden because no dwarfing rootstock is available and consequently they grow into large trees. Picking of what fruit has been left by the birds is difficult from a tall tree, and to ensure cross pollination two different varieties have to be planted. A fan-trained tree is the only feasible shape, and this requires sufficient wall space for two trees spaced 18–24ft apart. Even so, root pruning may be necessary in order to check vigour. However, birds can be kept from the fruit by draping netting over the tree.

The tree is built up in the same way as the peach (see page 109). Sweet cherries are pruned as little as possible once the framework is formed. Cut side shoots (laterals) back to five or six leaves in summer, then shorten these again to three or four leaves in the fall. Rub out shoots that appear on the wall side of the branches as soon as possible, while they are small. Branch tips (leaders) are not pruned until they reach the top of the wall when they are bent over and tied down for a year. This will weaken them and encourage new shoots to break so that the following fall the leaders can be cut back to replacement laterals. Also in the fall dead wood is removed and strong vertical shoots cut out, or tied down horizontally (which will weaken them) if they are needed to fill a gap.

Acid cherries　Acid cherries are not as vigorous as the sweet kinds and bush or fan trees can be planted in the garden about

105

15ft apart. They are more or less self-fertile and a single tree will set a good crop. The framework of bush trees is built up in the same way as for plums. Acid cherries fruit mainly on wood produced in the previous year, so once the framework of the tree has been formed subsequent pruning is aimed at encouraging this wood.

These cherries will make fresh growth from dormant buds in old wood, so each year a few branches are cut back to two-year-old wood in the case of young trees (about four or five years old), and into three- and four-year-old wood in the case of older trees. This is best done in spring after buds have burst. Diseased and dead wood is also removed, as well as inward and crossing branches to keep the head thinned out. Once again, paint large cuts with pruning wound dressing to prevent silver leaf infection.

Fan-shaped trees are built up in the same way as for peaches (page 109), except that only 3–4in is left between the side shoots. Once the tree is established a few of the older branches are cut back each year to encourage a supply of young shoots which are tied in 3–4in apart in winter. Otherwise pruning treatment is the same as for peaches.

9
Peaches

Peaches flower early and the danger is that the blossom is sometimes killed by frost, with consequent loss of fruit. To obtain some protection they are often grown trained in a fan-shape against a south- or west-facing wall. However, in a relatively frost-free situation free-standing trees can be grown with fair prospect of fruit.

Free-standing bushes

Training a free-standing bush is easy enough. When a one-year-old tree (a maiden) is planted, it is cut back late in the following spring to a suitable side shoot (lateral) 18–24in from the ground. Side shoots lower down the stem are removed entirely. In the following year there will be further side shoots which will compose the framework of branches. Cut these back by about one-third to an outward-facing bud. Shoots growing into the centre of the tree are removed and dead tips are cut back to a live bud.

The aim is to have branches arranged as evenly as possible in a spiral round the main stem. In subsequent years what pruning is necessary is carried out in spring. It is only necessary to tip-prune any shoots that have died back and to remove branches that are crossing others or crowding the centre of the tree. When old branches get pulled down to the ground by weight of fruit they are cut back in spring to a strong-growing vertical lateral.

Fan-trained trees

Trees are planted 9in away from a wall and the branches are tied to horizontal wires spaced about 6in apart so that they radiate like the spokes of a wheel. After planting in early spring a maiden tree is cut back to 24in from the ground. As shoots start to extend, one is left at the top plus a pair 8–9in above the ground and close together but on opposite sides of the stem. The other buds are rubbed out with the thumb. The two lower shoots are encouraged to grow along bamboo canes fixed to the wires and radiating out from the stem at an angle of 45°.

When the shoots are about 18in long the main stem above them is carefully cut out. If one shoot tends to grow more strongly than the other it must be brought down to a more horizontal position, which will restrain it.

In the second winter the two shoots are tied down to an even more horizontal position and cut back to about 18in. In the second summer a shoot at the end of each branch is allowed to grow along a cane to continue the growth of the main branch. Two shoots on the upper side of each branch are also allowed to grow, plus one on the lower side of each branch, and these are also tied to canes fixed to the wires. All other buds are rubbed out as soon as they can be handled.

In the third winter each new shoot is cut back by about one-third to a growth bud, on the upper side of the shoot if possible. Growth buds can be recognised because they are slender, while fruit buds are fat. If in doubt always cut to a triple bud cluster as these invariably consist of two fruit buds and one growth bud.

If there is space for a large tree, the treatment carried out in the second summer can be repeated once more, but otherwise steps are taken to secure a crop. To this end, third-summer treatment involves allowing the bud at the end of each of the eight branches to grow on, tying them to canes or directly to the wires. Rub out shoots that grow directly towards or away from the wall. Shoots from the remaining buds on both sides of the branch are kept where they can be spaced about 6in apart, and excess buds are rubbed out.

Once the shoots have grown to about 18in the tips are pinched out. They are tied to the wires so they are spaced

4–6in apart. These shoots should bear fruit the following year.

Fourth and subsequent summers require the removal of superfluous shoots, the pinching back of shoot tips and the tying-in of new shoots that will bear fruit in the following year. To obtain replacements for fruiting shoots, one shoot from a wood bud at the base is allowed to grow. Two shoots can be taken if there is a space to be filled. If the wall space is filled pinch new growths back to four leaves after six or seven have been formed.

Shoots close by a developing fruit are pinched back to two leaves. After the fruit has been gathered, fruit-bearing wood is cut off close to its replacement, which is then tied to the wires. Dead or diseased wood is removed at the same time.

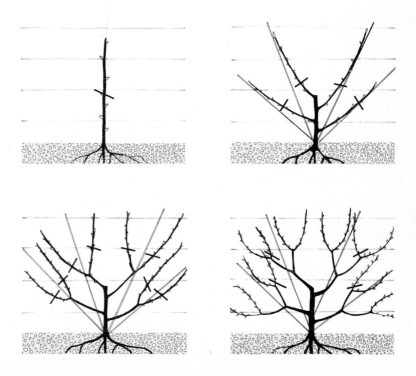

Stages in the shaping of a fan-trained tree, in its 1st, 2nd, 3rd and 4th years.

Pruning a peach. The sequence shows the reduction in the number of shoots. The final picture shows the end result, a fine crop of peaches.

10
Vines

It is easy to regard grapes as an exotic crop for the greenhouse, and to some extent this is true if large dessert berries are desired. But in many parts of the country, particularly regions in the south, a good crop can be obtained outdoors. If the right varieties are chosen these are usually excellent for eating and for wine-making.

Vines under glass

The easiest method is to train vines as single cordons, that is with a permanent single stem called a rod, from which side shoots grow each year and bear the bunches of grapes. As the best grapes grow on a current year's shoot, arising from the stub of one pruned the previous year, the pruning method has this end in view.

Young vines are usually planted just outside the greenhouse or conservatory and the main stem taken through a gap in the wall into the house. This is done to provide better conditions for the roots. If it is more convenient, the vine can be planted in the greenhouse but more watering will be required and this could be a problem during holidays.

A supporting system of horizontal wires is necessary. They must be 9in apart and at least 9in below the glass to avoid leaf scorching. The vine is planted in winter and cut hard back. The following growing season the strongest young shoot is allowed to grow up towards the apex of the house and the others are rubbed out. This leader will produce laterals (side

111

shoots) and these are pinched out at the tip when 18–24in long. Sub-laterals (side shoots from the laterals) are pinched when they have produced one leaf. It is important to space the laterals carefully so they are about 18in apart on alternate sides of the main stem. Badly placed or additional laterals must be removed while they are young enough to be rubbed out.

The vine will be ready for its first annual pruning when the leaves change colour in autumn, just before they fall. Although the rod may have reached the top of the greenhouse in the first year, it should be cut back to a bud where the shoot is well ripened. Cut back the laterals on the rod to one or two buds in order to build up a spur system. The following year one other shoot is allowed to continue extension growth until the roof area has been filled. Laterals are selected on alternate sides every 18in and stopped as before. Once this main shoot has grown to its maximum extent it is treated as a lateral.

Returning to the laterals that were cut back to spurs the previous autumn, these will produce new shoots in spring which, when 1–2in long, are reduced to two per spur by rubbing the rest out. If the lowest spurs are slow to produce new growths, spray the rod with warm water on sunny days, untie it from its supports and arch it down close to the ground until growth can be seen.

As they grow, tie the selected laterals to the framework of wires. Flower trusses will soon start to form on them, and further growth is then pinched out at two to four leaves beyond the truss. Sub-laterals are stopped at one leaf. It is usually necessary to reduce the number of bunches so that remaining grapes will swell to a good size. Some can be removed when the flowers are seen to have set, the remainder when the grapes have started to swell. As a guide, work to the formula of one bunch to 9in of rod. So that each bunch is not overcrowded, cut out some of the berries with a fine pointed pair of scissors. The remainder will be larger as a result. Of course, grapes for wine-making need not be thinned as much as those for the table.

The final job in the year's programme is to cut the laterals back to about two buds in autumn, leaving only short spurs along the main rod.

Vines outdoors

A south- or south-west-facing wall is an ideal place to grow a vine. A suitable shape is a fan tied to horizontal wires with two or three main rods carrying laterals. Training is the same as for vines under glass, except that initially two or three main shoots are allowed to grow. As before, a spur system is built up with laterals cut back close to the main rods in autumn.

The training method about to be described is suited to vines grown in rows – that is, without the support and protection of a wall – but the method can be adapted to wall training.

Vines supported in rows by wires can give good crops in many parts of the country if glass or polythene screens can be used to help ripening in late summer. The vines are planted 4ft 6in apart in a row running north–south or on a south-facing slope. Two wires are stretched along the row at 12in and 24in above the ground. Plants are set out during winter and cut hard back to encourage strong growths in summer. Three strong growths are enough and they will probably have to be cut back again in the second winter until the plant is well established and growing strongly. In the third winter two of the three shoots are bent down and trained along the lower wire. They are pruned back to between five and seven buds. The third shoot is cut back to three buds to produce three strong shoots for the following year.

The two shoots that have been spread out in opposite directions on the bottom wire and tied down will produce laterals from each bud. These will grow up to the top wire, to which they are tied. When the bunches of blossom are opening see that the fruiting laterals are stopped a few inches above the top wire by going down the row with shears.

If berry size is important, the bunches can be thinned when the grapes are swelling, leaving the best bunch on each lateral. Trimming with shears may be needed at intervals during the season to keep growth in check, and unwanted growths along the main stem and laterals should be rubbed out while small. The three replacement shoots are allowed to grow without stopping.

Glass or plastic panels along each side of the row in late summer will help ripening, but leave the top open for growth to come up and be trimmed back at intervals.

113

Pruning takes place once again after leaf fall when the two fruiting arms are untied from the lower wire and cut away close to the main stem, while two of the replacement canes are tied down in opposite directions to the lower wire and shortened as described above. Again, the third shoot is cut back to three buds for three new replacement shoots.

Vines can also be grown under large barn cloches, and pruning is largely the same except that only two new shoots are required each year. One wire only is needed, 9in above the ground. One shoot is shortened to eight buds and tied to the wire, while the other is cut back to two buds. These two buds will produce the replacement shoots. Cloches are put over the row in summer. Grapes are produced on the laterals that grow from the shoots tied to the wire. Stop these laterals at two leaves beyond the bunches.

11
Currants and Berries

Blackcurrant

Blackcurrant is an easy-to-grow and valuable bush fruit: valuable because it is one of the richest sources of vitamin C, while ease of culture extends to pruning. It also extends to propagating so that there is no excuse for keeping old and unfruitful bushes in the garden. Ten years is a good life for a blackcurrant bush, by which time it is likely to be much weakened by 'reversion' virus and the microscopic mite that helps to spread the trouble. Mites hatch within blackcurrant buds which appear abnormally big, giving rise to the condition called 'big bud'. The tissues in the bud are attacked by the mites and emerge distorted and unable to bear a decent crop of berries.

Control of big-bud mite by routine spraying also limits the spread of the virus, but pruning plays a significant part in the health of the blackcurrant by removal of quite substantial amounts of the oldest wood each year, thus disposing of pest colonies.

Cultivation of blackcurrants is forbidden in some US areas because the currants are host plants to a fungus that attacks white pines. Check with your co-operative extension service to see if you are in such an area before purchasing currant bushes.

Avoid at all costs the formation of a leg or stem on blackcurrant bushes. Foundations for a good shape are laid when the young bush is first planted by cutting the existing shoots back to 1in above the soil. Buds will break below these cuts and send up a cluster of shoots. In the autumn of the same year cut back half these young shoots, each close to soil-level.

Those remaining will bear fruit the following summer. They will also give rise to side shoots destined to fruit the year after, along with the regrowth from the cut-back shoots. In autumn again it is time to prune out a proportion of the shoots that have carried fruit. A reliable rule of thumb is to remove – by cutting out close to the soil – a quarter of the *old* wood each year.

It is tempting to make pruning cuts just above vigorous young growths that arise about halfway up the older wood. But if many cuts are made at this height the bush soon becomes tall, spindly and weakened as the supply of vigorous basal shoots on their own roots dwindles. So be firm and cut low: there will be ample renewal each year to replace the missing top growth. As well as old wood removal, encourage further suckering by cutting hard back about a quarter of the new basal growths each autumn. Pruning to this pattern will give the ideal balance of older and younger shoots.

It is possible to prune the blackcurrant while it is still in leaf without apparent detriment. Commercial growers commonly cut out the fruit-bearing shoots at picking time and take them away for stripping. This serves as pruning also, but such a ruthless approach is not recommended to gardeners.

Suckering and rooting near the soil surface is the aim, and is encouraged by laying mulches of straw, peat or rotted compost over the root area in early summer to keep the soil cool and moist. By the same token it is unwise to cultivate around the bushes and risk severing roots. Just remove weeds by hand if possible or hoe very superficially.

Red and white currants

Red and white currants are rarely seen in shops, which is good enough reason to grow them. Unlike the blackcurrant they are grown on a single stem or leg, and in this respect resemble the gooseberry, which also has similar pruning requirements. When cuttings of these currants are rooted, the buds on the bottom 6in of stem are rubbed or cut away to leave a clean leg. This will have been carried out on bushes purchased by the gardener. It is sufficient to keep four well-spaced shoots initially at the top of the stem, and to cut these back to three buds in the first winter. The following year a framework of about eight branches will be established.

Unlike the blackcurrant which fruits only on wood made the previous year, the red and white currants keep making fruit buds on the old wood year after year, so that old wood cannot be cut away without sacrificing a substantial amount of potential fruit. Suckers can arise from ground-level but are best torn away at the point of emergence in order to maintain a vase-shaped bush.

Many side shoots are made and these currant bushes will rapidly become a forest of growths unless pruned in summer as well as winter. This is done in late spring, shortening side shoots to within 3–4in of the main branches.

Winter pruning consists of cutting the side shoots back further, to two buds or half an inch. This is also the time to reduce the new growth at the top of the main branches. For the first couple of years reduce the new extension growth by a half, but as the bush matures be progressively more severe in limiting its height increase.

Birds like to eat unprotected buds on these currant bushes in winter, as well as sampling the fruit in summer, so it is wise to grow them within a bird-proof fruit cage.

To summarize the pruning process: preserve a clean stem or leg; establish a vase-shaped structure of about eight main branches; shorten back all side shoots in summer and again in winter, and tip prune leaders in winter. Allow for the occasional replacement of an original branch by a suitably placed younger one.

Red and white currants can be trained as cordon bushes to economize on space in the garden. Wires strained between posts are the ideal support. Set the bushes 1ft apart sloping at an angle of 45° and tied to a bamboo cane which is itself attached to the wires. Allow only one branch to grow as the leader, which should be tip-pruned back by one-third of its annual extension growth each winter. Prune all side shoots to 4in in summer, then cut back to $\frac{1}{2}$in in the winter. Fruit will form in a column on these spurs. Cordon currants are less attractive to birds because they do not provide a good 'footing'.

Gooseberry

Gloves are essential when tackling gooseberries with secateurs, and are also advisable at picking time. Garden bushes are grown on a clean stem or leg and, as with red currants, a semi-permanent framework of branches is established. However, the gooseberry fruits on both one- and two-year-old wood, so that removal of a proportion of old wood each year will not jeopardize fruiting.

If the bush is pruned on a replacement system rather like the blackcurrant, it is likely to fruit heavily but these fruits will tend to be small and most suitable for bottling. If, on the other hand, a spur-pruning system is adopted, such as was described for the red currant, there may be fewer fruits but they will be large and of dessert quality.

So, if size of berry is not important, winter-prune the bush by cutting out at a low level the older central wood in order to open up the bush and make picking easier. New growth on the chosen leading branches should be cut back by a half. Pruning for quality involves summer pruning of all side shoots to 4–5in, followed in winter by 'spurring back' to 2in. From then on, regrowth from these spurs is cut hard back to base. Limit the number of leader branches to a maximum of eight, and in winter cut back the annual extension growth by about a half. Gooseberry varieties that have a drooping habit should be leader-pruned to counteract this tendency. Always make the cuts on the leaders to an inward- and upward-pointing bud. As with red currants, birds will go for the buds in winter and it is best to keep gooseberries in a fruit cage.

The great advantage of cordon training for the gooseberry (apart from being space-saving) is that picking is made so much easier. Training and pruning follow the pattern already presented for red and white currants. It makes good sense to grow both types of fruit on the same framework.

Raspberry

Autumn is the best time to plant new raspberry canes. Once

118

Blackcurrants. These can be severely pruned as shown here. When cut to
ground-level they will produce plenty of young shoots, but will not usually
fruit well until the second year after this type of pruning.

planted they are pruned back to 1ft from the ground, cutting just above a bud. The following year these canes will be developing their root systems and sending up new canes (spawn). It is these that bear the first crop of berries the following summer.

It is best to provide raspberries from the outset with supporting wires stretched between posts. The first flush of new canes the summer after planting should not be pruned, although weak ones are best removed. The original canes are cut out at ground-level that autumn.

Regular pruning and thinning out begin in the second summer. More new canes than are required are produced along the row, and weak ones should be cut out or hoed away when they can be distinguished. Make a point of removing those furthest from the parent canes in order to keep the row narrow and easily supported. As a rule of thumb, keep six at the most from the group that has sprung from the parent root.

Treatment of canes that have carried fruit is simplicity itself. Cut them all out at ground-level soon after picking, and burn them as a precaution against spread of disease. Then, having selected and retained the best of the new canes, these are tied securely but not tightly to the wires. A continuous looping run of soft string is a good way to secure them.

Early spring is the time to tip-prune the new canes, removing the top 3in. This is done partly to remove damaged tips and partly to stimulate fruiting shoots below.

With the autumn-fruiting variety late fruit is borne on the current season's growth and new canes must be cut down to about 4in above ground in early spring.

Loganberry

A loganberry is generally trained in a fan-shape against a wall, fence or post-and-wire framework. After autumn planting existing cane is cut back to 9in above ground. Two or more new growths should arise at ground-level the following year. These are spaced and tied to horizontal wires with soft string. The following year these canes will bear fruit. The main pruning operation consists of their complete removal after picking.

The loganberry grows vigorously and a disciplined approach

to training is required to prevent it becoming unkempt. By the time the first fruit-bearing canes are cut away there will be a flush of new growths. The weakest can be removed at once and a maximum of eight strong ones tied down fan-wise on either side. Secure them so that the centre of the fan is left open to receive the following season's new growths. These in their turn will be lowered to re-form the fan when the older ones are cut out. This effectively separates old and young canes each year, and also ensures that the young growths are 'above' the old ones and so are less liable to be infected by any disease spored on the older parts.

In early spring tips of the canes which wave above the top wire (5–6ft high) are cut off. Growths that sprout an inconvenient distance from the parent root should be cut away at an early stage. These and blackberries are thorny subjects and gloves need to be worn during training and pruning operations. If planting for the first time take advantage of the thornless varieties of both fruit that are available and which are much easier to manage.

Blackberry

The pruning and training approach described for the loganberry can be applied to the blackberry—though this fruit is even more precocious in its annual growth and needs a firm hand to keep it within bounds. It bears fruit on the same wood for several years but it is best to cut out growths after they have fruited.

In the second year lead the fruiting canes up and along the higher wire of the supporting framework, while the new growths are grouped together and tied in at the bottom. In their turn a selection of these will be trained upwards when the older ones are removed at the base after fruiting.

Other hybrid berries

Certain hybrid berry fruits are offered by nurserymen, most of which are akin to the loganberry or blackberry, while others have currant *Ribes* in their 'blood'. Generally they are less hardy and less vigorous than their cousins. They may indeed be damaged by hard frost. Examples are the boysenberry,

121

youngberry and veitchberry. The wineberry is attractive in growth but has fruits of poor eating quality. Maintain a balance of fruiting and replacement growth in all cases.

A well-trimmed hedge is a joy at all seasons. Careful training is essential in the early years to achieve this sort of density.

12
Hedges

While the pruning of shrubs and fruit trees is a matter of choice —they will continue to 'perform' if let alone—it is a necessity with hedges, which must be tailored to shape. The term pruning is not often used by the gardener when he clips or trims the hedge, but that is what he is doing. The cuts are aimed at restricting or redirecting growth, and that is what pruning is all about.

A hedge is a barrier, or at least a demarcation. However low or slim, tall or spreading, its function is to separate one area from another—and to do it as harmoniously as possible. When kept under control a hedge is pleasing to the eye because it is a unity, the individual plants lost in a network of growth. Left untended, the unity that makes it a hedge is lost, and it resembles more a row of unkempt trees or shrubs too closely planted.

The degree of growth control varies greatly, however. More often than not a formal feature is desired which is regularly trimmed into a neat oblong shape, an elongated pyramid or a loaf of bread outline. A well-managed hedge of this type is evenly textured from ground to top. The opposite is not uncommon—a bare base, a matted middle and a sparse, spindly top.

The informal hedge, as the name implies, can be treated with more lax discipline. It is enough that growth should be fairly even. Flowering shrubs are chosen for informal hedges and are permitted to extend their flowering shoots naturally.

A well-maintained hedge will cost less than a fence or wall in the long term and will filter wind, so avoiding the dangerous turbulence caused by solid barriers. The effort of training is amply rewarded by the natural beauty.

Choice of hedging material is extensive, yet the majority of gardens still display only the well-known kinds. We do appear to live in a world subdivided by privet and cupressus, relieved by the occasional berberis. In fact the choice is wide enough to give great variety in height, leaf colour and texture, flower and berry. There are a large number of suitable 'evergreens'.

The approach to pruning is governed by the nature of the hedge. With small-leafed plants (which are chosen for formal hedges), overall trimming with shears or powered trimmer is the rule. When treated informally, however, pruning is more selective. With large-leafed subjects, such as laurel or rhododendron, prune with secateurs (pruning shears), because the effect of leaves severed by shears or clippers is unsightly and causes the leaf edges to discolour. There may be times when drastic measures are necessary in order to thin out and revive a hedge. At such times when old wood must be severed, a narrow-bladed saw is the best tool.

A basic rule relating to hedge shape is this: prune so that the bottom is wider than the top. This allows the whole surface area to get an equal share of light. All parts will then grow evenly and the base will not become bare.

Many gardeners, willing to use fertilizer and manure on other plants, neglect to feed hedges. This is a serious oversight for a hedge must occupy the same ground for many years and the mass of roots below the closely set plants make heavy demands on the food reserves of the soil. Only a well-nurtured hedge will respond properly to pruning, so dress the root area every two or three years with balanced organic or inorganic feeds applied in the spring. To reduce the risk of pest and disease infection be sure to clear away debris below the hedge each spring.

Begin pruning as soon as a newly planted hedge is established and making growth. To get the desired well-clothed base, clip off at least half the length of the new shoots three or four times each year until the young hedge is evenly dense. After this it will need attention once, twice or perhaps three times a year. It is the ubiquitous privet that demands the most trims. If privet and thorn are to look their best, three trims are needed, starting in early summer with follow-ups at six-week intervals. The relatively slow-growing yew and lonicera need several light trims if they are to keep a close 'finish'.

Summer is the time to give the single annual clip that is enough for a great number of hedging plants—beech among them. The table which follows summarizes the best available hedging subjects, and the pruning treatment for each is given in the following section.

Tools for hedge trimming must be in good condition. Shears that are blunt or out of alignment will tear growth and give an

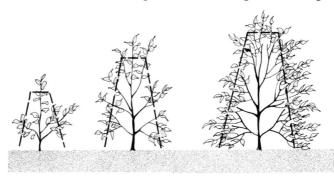

The shaping of a young hedge. The aim is to make the hedge narrower at the top than at the bottom. If the sides of the hedge are vertical the shoots at the base will not receive sufficient light to make enough dense growth.

unsatisfactory finish—to say nothing of leaving the gardener tired and frustrated from unrewarding effort. Likewise see that secateurs (pruning shears) cut evenly. Both can be professionally sharpened during the winter. A power-driven trimmer must be maintained as befits any electrical appliance, and great care taken in its use—especially if it is cable-trailing rather than battery powered.

Cutting a hedge straight by eye is not easy. A good aid is a tight line stretched between posts of equal height to indicate the topmost level of cut. On relatively short lengths, two canes alone pushed into the ground to equal height will suffice. A hedge tapering to a narrow top is the easiest shape to trim, as well as being best for growth. Always hold shears and power trimmer flat against the surface: never poke the tip into the hedge. Be sure to cut back long shoots that 'fill a gap'. Being cut they will branch and fill the gap better. Always shake the hedge to dislodge clippings, and clear them from the base.

How and when to prune hedges

Beech (*Fagus*)	trim to keep dense and regular in late summer or winter; brown leaves stay on through winter
Berberis darwinii	lightly after flowering in spring; flowers form berries later
Berberis stenophylla	lightly after flowering in spring; flowers form berries later
Berberis thunbergii atropurpurea	lightly to restore shape in winter (after autumn foliage effect)
Berberis thunbergii atropurpurea nana	does not exceed 2ft; trim in winter to maintain formal shape
Berberis thunbergii erecta	lightly in winter; makes a narrow hedge
Berberis verruculosa	lightly to restore shape after flowering in spring; flowers form berries later
Box (*Buxus*)	lightly as required in spring and summer
Chamaecyparis lawsoniana and forms	cut leading central shoot when desired height is reached. Trim in summer to limit spread
Cotoneaster lacteus	lightly to restore shape in summer, with regard to winter berry effect
Cotoneaster simonsii	trim this semi-evergreen lightly to shape in winter after berry and leaf effects have been enjoyed
Cupressocyparis leylandii	treat as for *Chamaecyparis* above
Cupressus macrocarpa	as above
Escallonia	lightly in spring, and again after flowering in summer to encourage more flowers. Except near the sea, frost may cut back this shrub
Euonymus japonica	use pruning shears to avoid unsightly cut leaves; lightly to maintain shape in spring
Griselinia	lightly in early summer; a tender shrub except near the sea
Hebe (*Veronica*)	trim to shape in spring; can be cut back hard if getting leggy
Holly (*Ilex*)	lightly to restore shape in late summer, with regard for winter berries. Cut back regularly when young to keep bushy at base
Hornbeam	as for beech above

126

Laurel	use secateurs (pruning shears) to avoid unsightly cut leaves; cut to maintain shape and density in spring
Lavender	lightly in spring, and cut off dead heads after flowering
Lonicera	frequently when young to achieve basal thickness; when mature, in spring and summer as required to maintain shape
Myrobalan plum	frequently when young to achieve basal thickness; when mature trim twice in summer
Olearia	lightly after flowering in summer
Osmarea	lightly after flowering in summer
Pittosporum	lightly to restore shape in spring or summer
Privet	frequently when young to achieve basal thickness; later as required during summer; rejuvenate by hard cutting-back in April
Prunus cistena	as below, but restrict new growth to 6in after flowering
Prunus pissardii	frequently when young to achieve basal thickness; when mature cut new growth well back to 18in after flowering in spring
Pyracantha rogersiana	lightly as flowers and fruit are carried on two-year-old wood; in spring after flowering
Quickthorn (*Crataegus*)	frequently when young to achieve basal thickness; when mature trim to shape in summer
Rhododendron ponticum	as little as possible with secateurs (pruning shears) to maintain outline; summer
Rosemary	lightly to shape in spring
Roses	hybrid teas and floribundas hard when young; moderately to maintain shape when mature. Shrub roses need old wood cut out at base and long shoots shortened to maintain shape; main pruning March, shoot shortening in summer
Santolina	lightly after flowering in spring
Sea Buckthorn	lightly in spring to maintain shape
Snowberry (*Symphoricarpus*)	lightly in spring with regard to winter berries
Syringa (*Lilac*)	as little as possible with secateurs (pruning shears) after flowering
Thuya	as for *Cupressus* above
Viburnum tinus	lightly in summer with secateurs (pruning shears)
Yew (*Taxus*)	trim to maintain shape in late summer; rejuvenate at base by hard cutting back

Name	low or high	formal or informal	'evergreen' or not	flower and fruit
Beech (*Fagus*)	H	F	semi E	–
Berberis darwinii	H	I	E	FF
Berberis stenophylla	H	I	E	FF
Berberis thunbergii atropurpurea	H	I	NE	–
Berberis thunbergii atropurpurea nana	L	F	NE	–
Berberis thunbergii erecta	L	F	NE	–
Berberis verruculosa	L	I	E	FF
Box (*Buxus*) (edging)	L	F	E	–
Box Handsworth	H	F	E	–
Chamaecyparis lawsoniana (forms *allumii* and *fletcheri* have bluish-grey foliage)	H	F	E	–
Cotoneaster lacteus	H	I	E	FF
Cotoneaster simonsii	H	I	semi E	FF
Cupressocyparis leylandii	H	F	E	–
Cupressus macrocarpa	H	F	E	–
Escallonia	H	F	semi E	Fl
Euonymus japonica (good variegated forms: attractive fruit on some)	H	F	E	–
Griselinia littoralis	H	F	E	–
Hebe (*Veronica*) species and varieties	L	I	E	Fl
Holly (*Ilex*)	H	F	E	Fr
Hornbeam (*Carpinus*)	H	F	semi E	–
Laurel, Portugal	H	F	E	FF
Lavender	L	F	E	Fl
Lonicera nitida	L	F	E	–
Myrobalan plum	H	I	NE	Fl
Olearia haastii	L	I	E	Fl
Osmarea burkwoodii	H	I	E	Fl
Pittosporum tenuifolium	H	I	E	–
Potentilla farreri	L	I	NE	Fl

Name	low or high	formal or informal	'evergreen' or not	flower and fruit
Privet (golden form also)	H	F	semi E	–
Prunus cistena (Crimson Dwarf)	L	F	NE	Fl
Prunus pissardii atropurpurea	H	I	NE	Fl
Prunus pissardii nigra (Blaze)	H	I	NE	Fl
Pyracantha rogersiana	H	I	E	FF
Quickthorn (*Crataegus*)	H	F/I	NE	FF
Rhododendron ponticum	H	I	E	Fl
Rosemary	L	F	NE	Fl
Rose, HT and Floribunda vars. esp. Queen Elizabeth	H	I	NE	Fl
Rose, species	H	I	NE	FF
Santolina chamaecyparissus	L	F	E	Fl
Sea Buckthorn (*Hippophae*)	H	I	NE	FF
Snowberry (*Symphoricarpus*)	H	I	NE	FF
Syringa (*Lilac*)	H	I	NE	Fl
Thuya plicata	H	F	E	–
Viburnum tinus (*Laurustinus*)	H	F	E	–
Yew (*Taxus*)	L/H	F	E	Fr

Key

Low	= under 4ft naturally
F	= formal (naturally regular or easily pruned to that shape)
I	= informal (looser habit, usually flowering)
E	= evergreen (but may apply to silver or other coloured foliage)
NE	= not evergreen, leaf losing in winter
semi E	= retain a proportion of foliage in fresh or dead state
FF	= flowering and fruiting
Fl	= flowers attractive
Fr	= fruit attractive

Index

130

132